Domestic Violence

ISSUES

Volume 108

Editor

Craig Donnellan

Independence

Educational Publishers
Cambridge

First published by Independence
PO Box 295
Cambridge CB1 3XP
England

British Library Cataloguing in Publication Data
Domestic Violence – (Issues Series)
I. Donnellan, Craig II. Series
362.8'292

ISBN 1 86168 328 6

Printed in Great Britain
MWL Print Group Ltd

Typeset by
Lisa Firth

Cover
The illustration on the front cover is by
Don Hatcher.

CONTENTS

Introduction

Domestic Violence is the one hundred and eighth volume in the **Issues** series. The aim of this series is to offer up-to-date information about important issues in our world.

Domestic Violence looks at contemporary issues relating to domestic abuse, the effect of domestic violence on young people through both their own experiences and observation of a parent's situation, and how and where to get help.

The information comes from a wide variety of sources and includes:
Government reports and statistics
Newspaper reports and features
Magazine articles and surveys
Website material
Literature from lobby groups
and charitable organisations.

It is hoped that, as you read about the many aspects of the issues explored in this book, you will critically evaluate the information presented. It is important that you decide whether you are being presented with facts or opinions. Does the writer give a biased or an unbiased report? If an opinion is being expressed, do you agree with the writer?

Domestic Violence offers a useful starting-point for those who need convenient access to information about the many issues involved. However, it is only a starting-point. At the back of the book is a list of organisations which you may want to contact for further information.

*****

Domestic abuse

An overview

What is domestic abuse?

Domestic abuse or domestic violence is the term used to describe any abusive behaviour within an intimate relationship between two people. Generally, people will first think of physical violence, such as hitting, beating and slapping, but domestic abuse also covers emotional, mental, verbal, sexual and financial behaviours perpetrated by one person on another within an intimate relationship. Abusive behaviour is used to exert control within a relationship.

Very rarely is one form of domestic abuse found by itself. Generally where one form of abuse exists, it is within the context of other forms of abuse. Hence a perpetrator of physical violence will also subject his victim to emotional and verbal abuse. Abuse rarely stays the same, but usually increases both in severity and frequency over a period of time.

In severe cases, domestic violence can lead to the victim of abuse being killed by the abuser. In other cases, the constant emotional and verbal abuse can slowly erode the victim's self-confidence and self-esteem. While physical abuse can, and often does, cause serious physical harm, often requiring medical intervention, emotional abuse hurts us deep inside and can leave permanent psychological and emotional scars.

Many people experience abuse within the so-called cycle of abuse or cycle of violence, in which periods of comparative calm or peace (known as the 'honeymoon stage') will be followed by a build-up toward an abusive episode. Though it may appear as though these periods of apparent calm are non-abusive, they are in actual fact simply part of a manipulative cycle, in which the abuser feels in control of their partner and situation, may show repentance for pain caused, even promise to change. Often it is these periods of apparent calm, which give the victim of abuse the hope that change can be achieved, and the abuse will stop, and keeps them locked in the abusive relationship.

The victims of abuse

Domestic abuse affects people from all social, racial and financial backgrounds. It affects men and women, old and young, heterosexual couples and homosexual couples alike. It may start almost immediately, or only after several years of being in a relationship. Though both victims and perpetrators of abuse come from all backgrounds, the shock, pain, confusion, feelings of guilt and betrayal of trust experienced as a result of being subject to domestic violence is common to all.

Many sufferers of violence do not speak out about what is happening at home, but suffer in silence, often for years. They may try to deny it to themselves, not wanting to admit to the reality of the abuse; they may feel shame about the abuse, as though it were their fault. A feeling of guilt about the abuse is almost universal – the victim of abuse believing, and being told by the perpetrator, that they or their actions are the cause of the abuse. This has a double effect: it enables the abuser to continue to feel justified in continuing their destructive behaviour, as the victim takes responsibility for the abuse, and also allows the victim to continue to believe that they can change the situation and can in some way control the abuse and stop it. Real change in a perpetrator of abuse however is sadly very rare.

Above all, it needs stressing that the victim of abuse is not responsible for the abuse and violence, but is being manipulated and coerced by the perpetrator.

Some long-term effects of abuse

While it seems obvious that physical violence can result in long-term effects and even disability (if not death), the consequences of suffering ongoing emotional abuse are often overlooked or minimised. As stated earlier on, emotional abuse can affect us deep inside and leave permanent emotional and psychological scars.

Those who have been abused often experience long-term feelings and reactions, which can cause a lot of distress, including flashbacks, sudden feelings of anxiety, an inability to concentrate or feelings of unreality. These reactions and feelings are a normal reaction to a traumatic event and in their extreme form – especially where accompanied by depression and suicidal ideation – are considered Post-Traumatic Stress Disorder (PTSD), which requires medical assistance and support.

Even where the abuse does not have physical long-term effects or result in PTSD, the survivor of an abusive relationship will often suffer low self-esteem and feelings of worthlessness. Survivors commonly comment on feeling somehow 'different' to their peers, as though their experiences have in some way set them apart from the rest of society. Due to the controlling aspects of an abusive relationship, the survivors may find it difficult to make personal decisions and easily feel overwhelmed by everyday tasks. Throughout the abusive relationship, the victim of abuse will use various different coping mechanisms to survive emotionally and physically which are a necessary strategy while in such a situation, but can be debilitating in a non-abusive environment, and these have to be unlearned. Since abuse and violence within an intimate relationship are also a huge betrayal of trust, the survivor of abuse will often also have difficulty learning to trust someone else and open up emotionally for fear of being betrayed again.

Why are some people abusive?

It would be nice to know that all abusers walk around with a big A for 'abuser' on their forehead, are easily discernable by anyone 'normal' and always comply with the stereotypical image so often portrayed in the media. In actual fact one of the main problems encountered by victims, friends, family and various agencies dealing with the consequences of an abusive relationship, is how 'normal' the abuser seemed. Many victims of abuse comment on how their partner is like a 'Jekyll and Hyde' – seems

fine and lovely one moment or in public, but presents a completely different personality in private or at a different time. Often the victim of abuse will spend hours trying to work out what is causing the abuse, what makes their partner abusive.

Some people believe that abuse is only a case of bad anger management on the part of the perpetrator, and no doubt in some cases the abuser does have a problem dealing with anger in a non-destructive manner, but on the whole the reasons or causes of abuse are much more deep-rooted and complicated than a problem with anger or bad moods. There are various theories which try to explain why abuse takes place, including the theory that abuse is due to our living in a patriarchal society in which men perceive themselves as having a born right to control women and believe them to be their inferiors. This, however, does not explain why abuse should occur within homosexual relationships, nor why in some cases it is the woman who is abusive toward her male partner. Another theory holds that abuse is a learned behaviour, i.e. that children who witness abuse at an early stage, will automatically go on to be abusive themselves, and while this does hold true for some perpetrators, the majority of abused children do not go on to abuse their partners in adulthood, nor does it explain why some adults from apparently non-abusive homes

should carry on to become abusive themselves.

What is clear is that most abusers do not have feelings of either good self-esteem or self-worth themselves and feel the need to control their environment to feel in control (safe and secure) themselves. Where their attempts to control another person are successful, this abusive behaviour and belief in the ability to control their environment is increased – hence the chances of them changing are theoretically decreased the longer the abusive relationship continues.

Most abusers do not have feelings of either good self-esteem or self-worth themselves

---

In some cases abusive behaviour can be the result of mental illness, for instance someone suffering from schizophrenia may be violent toward their loved ones or destroy their belongings.

Someone suffering from a dissociative disorder (DID) may also act out in a violent manner or be emotionally abusive. While the effects on the victim can be equally damaging or lethal, this abuse has to be considered within the context of the illness rather than specifically within the context of an abusive relationship as such.

Frequency of domestic violence

Frequency of domestic violence from the perpetrator of the worst incident of domestic violence among those who have ever been victims since the age of 16

Source: Figure 2.4, Home Office Research Study 276 – Domestic violence, sexual assault and stalking: Findings from the British Crime Survey. Crown Copyright 2004.

Is it possible to spot a potential abuser?

While not all abusers act in the same way, it is sometimes possible to predict the likelihood of the person you are currently or are about to become involved with being abusive, since many, if not most, display some common tendencies. These may include excessive jealousy, controlling behaviour (often disguised or excused as concern), quick involvement and pressuring their boy/girlfriend to commit to them early on. They may have unrealistic expectations from either their partner or the relationship itself, may try to isolate their partner from family, friends or other social interactions, and are often hypersensitive, getting easily hurt or offended. Very rarely will an abusive person accept responsibility for any negative situation or problem, but will tend to shift the responsibility onto other people or situations in general. In a similar way, abusers will shift the blame/cause of their feelings outside of themselves, seeing their emotions as a reaction to other people or situations rather than stemming from themselves.

Abusers will shift the blame/cause of their feelings outside of themselves, seeing their emotions as a reaction to other people or situations

---

Other warning signs may include cruelty toward animals and/or children, the 'playful' use of force in sex, threats of violence or punishment, a belief in rigid stereotypical gender roles in a relationship, force used during an argument, and breaking or smashing objects.

While these potential warning signs may be helpful, the best defence against ending up as a victim of abuse may be to maintain a strong sense of self and one's personal boundaries, while at the same time realising that if one does find oneself in an abusive relationship, it is not one's own fault, and there is help available to escape.

How to help a friend experiencing abuse

If a friend confides in you that they are experiencing abuse, there are various ways in which you can help them. Here are a few suggestions:

- Believe what they are telling you and be understanding – the chances are that you are hearing only about of the tip of the iceberg.
- Inform yourself as much as possible about domestic abuse/violence and the resources available to victims and survivors – check out the web, local libraries and health centres, etc.
- Be supportive toward your friend, reassure them that the abuse is not OK and not something they have to put up with, but don't try to tell them what to do about it, let them make their own decisions knowing that you will be there for them regardless of their choice at that moment in time, even if it is staying with their abuser.
- You can provide practical assistance by accompanying them to their GP or local hospital if your friend is hurt and needs medical assistance, or by offering your address for info packs or your telephone for phone calls.
- Help your friend to plan a safe strategy for leaving, bearing in mind that they will know what is and what is not safe, while ensuring that you don't pressurise them into doing something which they may have doubts about.
- Remember to look after yourself while supporting your friend!

If you are suffering abuse

If you are being abused, please realise that it is not your fault, that you are not to blame for the abuse and violence and that there is very little hope of the abuser changing. Know that there are many others who have experiences similar to yours and have survived, and that there is help and support available to you.

Look after yourself and treat yourself as your friend. Learn as much as you can about abuse and don't be frightened of seeking support and help.

Where to find help and support in the UK

If you are living in the UK you can call the National Domestic Violence Helpline on 08457 023468, which will provide a confidential listening ear and advice. If you are in need of immediate assistance and somewhere to go, call Refuge's 24-hour National Crisis Line on 0990 995 443.

The Women's Aid National Domestic Violence Helpline is also available to offer support, information and advice on what to do or where to go on 0345 023 468.

Male victims of abuse can call the Men's Advice Line and Enquiries on 020 8644 9914 for information, support and advice to men experiencing domestic violence.

For more national and regional helplines, check out the Resources section of Hidden Hurt, while a complete up-to-date list of Women's Aid and National Refuge numbers is available at www.womensaid.org.uk

Other sources of help, support and advice can be found in your local telephone book or Yellow Pages, local library and obviously via your GP, local council offices and Social Services departments.

Many Refuges offer local support groups for both victims and survivors of domestic abuse and these can be found by contacting your local Refuge (see Womens' Aid website or phone 0345 023 468).

- Reprinted with kind permission from Hidden Hurt – please visit www.hiddenhurt.co.uk for more or see page 41 for address details.
© Hidden Hurt

Facts about domestic violence

One in four women experience domestic violence in their life...

Domestic violence happens to a lot of women and children, and also to some men – in the UK and all across the world. Here are some facts about domestic violence. Check out the links to other sites in the 'More help' section on our website for more information.

- 1 in 4 women experience domestic violence in their life and between 1 in 6 to 1 in 10 women suffer domestic violence every year. (Council of Europe, 2002)
- In the 2001/02 British Crime Survey, 89% of the people who experienced more than four incidents of domestic violence were women. (Home Office, 2004)
- The 2001/02 British Crime Survey found that more than half (57%) of victims of domestic violence experience violence on more than one occasion. (Home Office, July 2002)
- The 2001/02 British Crime Survey found that there were an estimated 635,000 incidents of domestic violence in England and Wales. 81% of the victims were women and 19% were men. (Home Office, July 2002)
- Nearly one-half (45%) of women who responded to the 2001/02 British Crime Survey and one-quarter (26%) of men reported being victim of either domestic violence, sexual assault or stalking. (Home Office, 2004)

THE HIDEOUT
www.thehideout.org.uk
until children are safe

- Every minute in the UK, the police receive a call for help for domestic violence. This means the police receive about 1,300 calls about domestic violence each day or over 570,000 each year. (Stanko, 2000)
- At least 750,000 children a year witness domestic violence. Nearly three-quarters of children on the child protection register live in households where domestic violence occurs. (Department of Health, 2003)
- One woman is killed every two days by a current or former partner. (Criminal Statistics, Home Office, 1995)
- 1 in 5 young men and 1 in 10 young women think that abuse or violence against women is acceptable. (Zero Tolerance Charitable Trust, 1998)
- Depending on the study, researchers estimate that in 30-66% of domestic violence cases, the abuser is also abusing the children in the family. (Hester et al, 2000; Edleson, 1999) (Humphreys & Thiara, 2002)

- An estimated 18,569 women and 23,084 children stayed in refuges in England during the year 2003/04. (Women's Aid, 2005)
- In 2003/04 142,526 women and 106,118 children received support for domestic violence in England. (Women's Aid, 2005)
- Approximately 2/3 of the people staying in refuges in England are children. (Women's Aid, 2005)
- An estimated 156 disabled women and 61 disabled children received support for domestic violence in England on the Women's Aid census day, 2 November 2004. (Women's Aid, 2005)
- On the Women's Aid census day (2 November 2004) approximately 45% of children staying in refuges were under the age of 5, 39% of children were between the ages of 5 and 10 and 16% were between the ages of 11 and 16. (Women's Aid, 2005)

- The Hideout is the first national website to support children and young people living with domestic violence, or those who may want to help a friend. The Hideout (www.thehideout.org.uk) informs children and young people about domestic violence and helps them identify whether it is happening in their home.

Reproduced with kind permission from Women's Aid.

Types of abuse

Information from Hidden Hurt

We tend to think of domestic abuse as physical violence or assault on a wife. In reality, however, domestic abuse is the summary of physically, sexually and psychologically abusive behaviours directed by one partner against another, regardless of their marital status or gender. Generally, when one form of abuse exists, it is coupled with other forms as well.

Domestic abuse may also be defined by identifying its function, that being the domination, punishment or control of one's partner. Abusers use physical and sexual violence, threats, money, emotional and psychological abuse to control their partners and get their way.

Physical abuse

Physical assault is the most obvious form of domestic violence, the most visible, and also the most lethal. Assaults often start small, maybe a small shove during an argument, or forcefully grabbing your wrist, but over time, physical abuse (or battering) usually becomes more severe, and more frequent, and can result in the death of the victim.

Physical abuse is any act of violence on the victim, and can include the following:

- slapping,
- kicking,
- shoving,
- choking,
- pinching,
- forced feeding,
- pulling hair,
- punching,
- throwing things,
- burning,
- beating,
- use of weapons (gun, knives, or any object)
- physical restraint – pinning against wall, floor, bed, etc.
- reckless driving, etc.

Basically any behaviour which hurts or physically harms, or is intended to do so.

Threats

Where threats are made within a violent relationship they can be as debilitating as the violence itself. A victim who has already suffered being battered need not imagine the result of displeasing the abuser, or doubt the abuser's ability to carry out the threats. Even where the victim has not been physically assaulted, the abuser will often demonstrate his ability to harm her by punching walls or furniture, kicking the cat/dog, or using aggressive behaviour.

Abusers use physical and sexual violence, threats, money, emotional and psychological abuse

However, many threats are not physical but part of the ongoing emotional abuse. The abuser may threaten to 'disappear' with the children, report his partner to Social Services as an unfit mother, harm a significant third party (e.g. family member), refuse housekeeping, leave or commit suicide. Whether the threats are of a physical, sexual or emotional nature, they are all designed to further control the victim by instilling fear and ensuring compliance. The abuser becomes not only the source of pain and abuse, but also the protector, as he is also the person who can prevent the threatened action, increasing the victim's dependence on him.

Sexual abuse

Sexual abuse can be defined as any sexual encounter without consent and includes any unwanted touching, forced sexual activity, be it oral, anal or vaginal, forcing the victim to perform sexual acts, painful or degrading acts during intercourse (e.g. urinating on victim), and exploitation through photography or prostitution.

The abuser may use violence to rape his partner (this is most common where physical violence is also current) or he may use only enough force to control his partner's movements (known as 'force-only rape'). Coercion or manipulation in the form of threats, emotional or psychological abuse may also be used, leaving the victim to submit to unwanted sexual acts out of fear or guilt. The abuser may, for instance, imply that should she not submit, he will hit her, leave her and find 'another woman', withdraw the housekeeping, or punish her in some other way. Or the abuser may insist on sex following a physical attack for the victim to 'prove' she has forgiven him. Whatever form of coercion is used, be it physical, financial or emotional, any sexual act which is not based on mutual consent constitutes sexual abuse.

The wheel of power and control

Abusers believe they have a right to control their partners by:
- Telling them what to do, expecting obedience
- Using force to maintain power and control over partners
- Feeling their partners have no right to challenge their desire for power and control
- Feeling justified making the victim comply
- Blaming the abuse on the partner and not accepting responsibility for wrongful acts.

The characteristics shown in the wheel are examples of how this power and control are demonstrated and enacted against the victim.

Source: Wheel of Abuse provided courtesy of Kim Eyer of rhiannon3.org

Sexual abuse can involve any of the following:

- excessive jealousy
- calling you sexually derogatory names
- criticising you sexually
- forcing unwanted sexual act
- forcing you to strip
- sadistic sexual acts
- withholding sex and/or affection
- minimising or denying your feelings about sex or sexual preferences
- forcing sex after physical assault
- using coercion to force sex
- taking unwanted sexual photos
- forcing you into prostitution
- forcing sex when you are ill or tired.

Marital rape

When sexual abuse occurs within marriage, the victim will often feel very confused as to whether or not she has been 'raped'. It seems obvious to all (general public, law enforcement agencies, religious leaders, etc.) that when a woman (or man) is raped out on the street by a stranger, that rape has occurred and is wrong. When rape occurs within the marriage, neither abuser nor victim may consider it legal rape. This is partially due to the general acceptance of the Christian tradition within our culture which tells us that it is the wife's duty to fulfil her husband's sexual demands. Many women (both religious and non-religious) don't believe they have the right to refuse sex, that 'sex on demand' is an unwritten part of the marriage contract. When they have been raped by their husband, they are inclined to take responsibility for the abuse, furthering the feelings of guilt and lack of self-worth. This blame-taking is further increased by the abuser's justifications, e.g. 'it is your fault for saying no . . .'. When no actual physical violence was used (i.e. coercion or force-only), many men will deny that rape has actually occurred and treat the abuse as though it was normal and by joint consent. This has the effect of further confusing the victim as to the reality of her experience.

Marriage, however, is a contract based on mutual love, respect and consideration. Each party has a right to their own body, and while consideration for each person's sexual needs is normal, forced sexual acts are not an expression of love, but a purposeful betrayal of the respect and trust which form a solid marriage.

Emotional/psychological abuse

Many forms of abuse are obviously cruel. Emotional abuse is more subtle. Quite often such abuse goes unseen, as even the victim does not recognise that she is being abused. Although emotional abuse does not leave black eyes or visible bruises, it is often more seriously damaging to your self-esteem. Emotional abuse is cruel and scars your soul. Physical or sexual abuse is always accompanied and often follows emotional abuse, i.e. emotional battering is used to wear the victim down – often over a long period of time – to undermine her self-concept until she is willing to take responsibility for her abuser's actions and behaviour towards her or simply accept it.

There are many categories of emotional/psychological abuse. They encompass a variety of behaviours that will be easily recognisable by those experiencing them, and often remain completely unnoticed by others. They include:

Isolation

The abuser will control whom the victim sees, where she goes, whom she speaks to and what she does. This can take the form of simply not allowing her to use the phone, have her friends round or visit her family, or ensuring it simply isn't worth it by being in a bad mood because she left some housework undone, making her feel guilty that she was out enjoying herself while he worked, or even encouraging her – theoretically – to make friends, and then discounting them or complaining that she cares more for her friends/family/hobby than she does for him or is neglecting him. Some abusers may move home frequently to prevent their victim from building a social support network.

Many abusers justify their control over their victim by stating that it is proof of their love, or that they worry about their safety when out, etc. In reality, however, the abusers need to isolate their victims to feel secure themselves, they feel as though any relationship, be it family, friend or colleague, will undermine their authority over and take their partner away from them, i.e. poses a threat. The effect of this isolation is that the victim feels very alone in her struggle, doesn't have anyone with whom to do a 'reality check', and is ultimately more dependent on the abuser for all her social needs.

Forms of isolation include:

- checking up on you
- accusing you of unfaithfulness
- moving to an isolated area
- ensuring you lack transport or a telephone
- making your friends or family feel uncomfortable when visiting so that they cease
- punishing you for being 10 minutes late home from work by complaining, bad moods, criticism or physical abuse
- not allowing you to leave the house on your own
- demanding a report on your actions and conversations
- preventing you from working
- not allowing any activity which excludes him

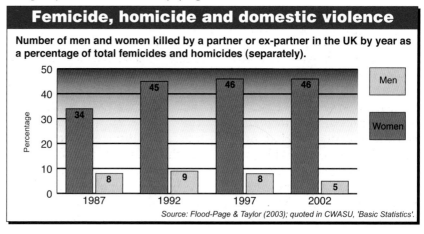

Femicide, homicide and domestic violence

Number of men and women killed by a partner or ex-partner in the UK by year as a percentage of total femicides and homicides (separately).

Year	Men	Women
1987	8	34
1992	9	45
1997	8	46
2002	5	46

Source: Flood-Page & Taylor (2003); quoted in CWASU, 'Basic Statistics'.

- finding fault with your friends/ family
- insisting on taking you to and collecting you from work.

In extreme cases the victim may be reduced to episodes of literally becoming a prisoner, being locked in a room and denied basic necessities, such as warmth, food, toilet or washing facilities.

Verbal abuse

When thinking of verbal abuse we tend to envisage the abuser hurling insulting names at the victim, and while this obviously does happen, there are many more forms than name-calling. The abuser may use critical, insulting or humiliating remarks (e.g. you've got a mind like ditchwater; you're stupid; etc.), he may withhold conversation and refuse to discuss issues, or he may keep you up all night insisting on talking when you need sleep. Verbal abuse undermines your sense of worth, your self-concept (i.e. who you think you are) by discounting your ideals, opinions or beliefs.

Verbal abuse can include:
- yelling or shouting at you
- making threats
- insulting you or your family
- being sarcastic about or criticising your interests, opinions or beliefs
- humiliating you either in private or in company

Verbal abuse undermines your sense of worth, your self-concept, by discounting your ideals, opinions or beliefs

- sneering, growling, name-calling
- withholding approval, appreciation, or conversation
- refusing to discuss issues which are important to you
- laughing or making fun of you inappropriately
- leaving nasty messages
- accusing you of unfaithfulness, not trying hard enough or purposely doing something to annoy
- blaming you for his failures or other forms of abuse.

All of these abusive behaviours prohibit normal, healthy interaction between two adults as well as showing a lack of respect for individual thoughts, feelings, and opinions. A healthy, mutual interaction and conversation between two persons respects and promotes the right of each partner to their own individual thoughts, perceptions and values.

Financial abuse

Financial abuse can take many forms, from denying you all access to funds, to making you solely responsible for all finances while handling money irresponsibly himself. Money becomes a tool by which the abuser can further control the victim, ensuring either her financial dependence on him, or shifting the responsibility of keeping a roof over the family's head onto the victim while simultaneously denying your ability to do so or obstructing you.

Financial abuse can include the following:
- preventing you from getting or keeping a job
- denying you sufficient housekeeping
- having to account for every penny spent
- denying access to cheque book/ account/finances
- putting all bills in your name
- demanding your pay cheques
- spending money allocated to bills/ groceries on himself
- forcing you to beg or commit crimes for money
- spending Child Benefit on himself
- not permitting you to spend available funds on yourself or children.

- Information from Hidden Hurt – visit www.hiddenhurt.co.uk, or see page 41 for address details.

© Hidden Hurt

Myths and facts

Common misunderstandings about domestic violence

Half of all homicides of women are killings by a partner or ex-partner

'If the violence/abuse was really serious, the women would report it'
Domestic violence is a violent crime, which regularly leads to hospitalisation and death. Half of all homicides of women are killings by a partner or ex-partner. One study found that 46% of women who suffer violence did not report because they feared reprisals, and many think that they will not be believed or taken seriously.

'If the violence/abuse were really serious, she would leave'
Many women have been subject to regular threats by their partner that if she leaves he will find her and kill her. Some men also threaten to kill the children. Women believe these threats, and they are justified in doing so, since research now shows that the most dangerous time for women is when they have left or decided to leave – this is the time when most domestic homicides occur.

Fear is the strongest factor that prevents women from leaving – leaving safely requires protection. For migrant women their 'right to stay' in the country may be linked to their partner, meaning they risk deportation if they leave.

But there are other reasons that women stay – they often care about their partner, and not all violent men are the same. Some of them are not violent all the time, and after each incident are apologetic and promise to change. In these kinds of relationships women tend to live in the good times and forget or minimise the bad times. Where the violence is made worse by alcohol, drugs or a health problem, the woman may believe that if only they can sort out this problem, then the violence will stop.

And again we should not forget that many women do end relationships with violent partners. But doing so often involves considerable costs and losses – of financial security, one's home, possessions and familiar surroundings. These are not decisions anyone takes lightly. It is not surprising, therefore, that most women leave and return several times, in hope or in fear, before they manage to get away for good.

It is even harder in a context where the woman is economically dependent, does not have employment or qualifications and where there is minimal, if any, financial assistance and social welfare provision. In some European countries it is virtually impossible for a woman on her own to find housing. Provision of shelters is scarce in many countries and demand almost always exceeds supply of even this minimal resource.

'Violent men are usually drunk or they grew up in violent households'

Whilst there is some strong evidence, especially from some countries, that domestic violence is linked to alcohol, it is not alcohol which causes the violence. This is both because most men are also abusive when they are sober and because most men are not generally violent when drunk – they only assault their partner and children, usually behind closed doors.

Some violent men did grow up in families in which domestic violence happened – but some did not. Not all boys growing up with it now will choose to become abusers. And this is the important key here – it is always a choice to use violence.

These ideas are popular because they allow us to think that only certain men are violent. It is hard to accept that violent men are 'normal': the man next door, a friend or colleague

even. Many men hold firm beliefs that what goes on in their own home is their own business or that women should know their place. You may not be aware that they are violent, may never have seen them angry. This is one of the reasons why women can find it hard to get help or support – if their husband is known, liked or respected by friends and family, and sometimes the wider community, who will believe her?

Stereotypes about violent men are both inaccurate and dangerous: they can prevent us from keeping an open mind and put women and children's lives at risk.

Many men hold firm beliefs that what goes on in their own home is their own business

'Only certain groups or types of women are abused'

Again this is a comfortable view, which suggests that domestic violence is limited to certain groups or 'types' of women. Traditionally the idea has been that disadvantaged groups are the ones in which violence is common, but prevalence surveys show that domestic violence takes place across class, race, age and social status. However, in the 1990s researchers and activists (see for example Kanuha, 1996) began to

explore whether higher incidence rates do exist among particular groups of women.

'The violence is often a one off: a row gone a bit too far'

If it is a single incident then it is not domestic violence. Domestic violence involves ongoing abuse, which invariably becomes more frequent and more dangerous over time. It is important for professionals not to assume that just because this is the first incident they are aware of, that this means it is the first time violence has been used. Very few women call the police or contact other organisations following the first incident.

'There's little point in intervening, the couple usually sort it out themselves'

The couple very rarely sort it out themselves. The more common pattern is for violence to continue and escalate – doing more damage to women and children in the process. Police officers have a duty to intervene not only to enforce the law, but also to ensure that perpetrators do not think they can continue with impunity, and to communicate to women and children that they have the right to live free from violence. Other agencies and community members have a responsibility not to ignore violence and abuse, to offer sanctuary to women and children, and to challenge abusive men.

'People should not interfere in private affairs'

This has been one of the strongest reasons used over the years for not getting involved in domestic violence. It does indeed occur in the private sphere – although not always, some women are assaulted in public, and stalked at work or when they have moved to another home.

■ Reprinted with kind permission from the Child and Women Abuse Studies Unit – visit www.cwasu.org for more information or see page 41 for address details.
© London Metropolitan University

The extent of domestic violence

Findings from the British Crime Survey

Experience of domestic violence in the 12 months prior to interview

- Four per cent of women and two per cent of men were subject to domestic violence (non-sexual domestic threats or force) during the last year. Extending the definition to include financial and emotional abuse increases these figures to six and five per cent respectively. If the definition of domestic violence is narrowed to non-sexual domestic force only, then three per cent of women and two per cent of men were affected.

- Among women subject to domestic violence (non-sexual threats or force) in the last year, the average number of incidents was 20, while 28 per cent experienced one incident only. Of men subject to domestic violence (non-sexual threats or force) in the last year, the (mean) average number of incidents was seven, while one incident was experienced by 47 per cent.

- There were an estimated 12.9 million incidents of domestic

violence acts (non-sexual threats or force) against women and 2.5 million against men in England and Wales in the year prior to interview.

Lifetime and since age 16 experience of domestic violence

- The BCS estimates that one in five (21%) women and one in ten (10%) men have experienced at least one incident of non-sexual domestic threat or force since they were 16. If financial and emotional abuse are included, then 26 per cent of women and 17 per cent of men had experienced domestic violence since the age of 16.

The most heavily abused

- Women are the overwhelming majority of the most heavily abused group. Among people subject to four or more incidents of domestic violence from the perpetrator of the worst incident (since age 16), 89 per cent were women. Thirty-two per cent of women had experienced domestic violence from this person four or more times compared with only 11 per cent of men.

The experience of domestic violence: impact and meaning

The following findings refer to the worst incident (victim defined) experienced in the time period specified.

- Injuries were often sustained as a result of domestic violence, especially among women. During the worst incident of domestic violence experienced in the last year, 46 per cent of women sustained a minor physical injury, 20 per cent a moderate physical injury, and six per cent severe

injuries, while for 31 per cent it resulted in mental or emotional problems. Among men, 41 per cent sustained a minor physical injury, 14 per cent a moderate physical injury, one per cent severe injuries and nine per cent mental or emotional problems.

- Domestic violence has a detrimental impact on employment. Among employed women who suffered domestic violence in the last year, 21 per cent took time off work and two per cent lost their jobs. Among men in this situation, six per cent took time off work and two per cent lost their jobs.

- 64 per cent of women and 94 per cent of men subject to domestic violence in the last year did not think that what had happened to them was a crime. However, two-thirds of women who had been victimised many times did think it was a crime. These women were also more likely to think that what had happened to them was 'domestic violence'. There was a greater likelihood of applying the concepts of domestic violence and crime to the incident if injuries were sustained and the acts were severe and repeated.

Offenders and relationships

- Leaving their violent partner led to the cessation of the domestic violence for the majority (63%) of women; for a significant minority (18%) it continued in another form, such as stalking or harassment. For 78 per cent of men who left the violent partner the violence stopped.

- Of the female victims of domestic violence who had seen the perpetrator since they had split up because of their children, 29 per cent had been threatened, 13 per cent had been abused in some way, two per cent had had their children threatened, and in one per cent of cases the perpetrator had hurt the children.

Risk factors

■ During the last year women in households with an income of less than £10,000 were three and a half times more likely to suffer domestic violence than those living in households with an income of over £20,000, while men were one and a half times more likely. The nature of the links between poverty and risk of interpersonal violence is unclear. It may be that poverty is associated with the onset of domestic violence, or it may be that in fleeing domestic violence women are reduced to poverty.

Seeking help

■ Thirty-one per cent of female victims and 63 per cent of male victims had not told anyone other than the survey about the worst incident of domestic violence that they had suffered during the last year.

■ Asked why they did not report the worst incident of domestic violence in the last year, 41 per cent of women and 68 per cent of men replied they thought that it was too trivial, 38 per cent of women and 39 per cent of men that it was a private family matter, seven per cent of women and five per cent of men that they did not want any more humiliation, and 13 per cent of women, but no discernible percentage of men, that they feared more violence or that the situation would get worse as a result of police involvement.

■ In the worst cases of domestic violence against women during the last year where the police had been informed, as far as the women were aware, the police had arrested the perpetrator in 21 per cent of cases, sent him to court in 10 per cent, spoken to him in 42 per cent of cases, and, in 29 per cent of cases, not found the person, nor spoken to or arrested him, nor sent him to

court. Of that minority of women who used the police service, 68 per cent were fairly or very satisfied and 31 per cent a bit or very dissatisfied.

■ Of those who suffered injuries in the worst incident of domestic violence in the last year, 27 per cent of women and 14 per cent of men sought medical assistance on that occasion. Of the women who sought medical assistance, 94 per cent were asked the cause of their injuries by the attending doctor or nurse, 74 per cent

disclosed a cause, and only 26 per cent were referred on to someone else who could help them.

■ The above information is an extract from the summary of the report *Home Office Research Study 276: Domestic violence, sexual assault and stalking: Findings from the British Crime Survey*. To read the full report or for more information, please visit the Home Office's website at www.homeoffice.gov.uk

The cost of domestic violence

Key findings from the Department of Trade and Industry

The total cost of domestic violence to services (criminal justice system, health, social services, housing, civil legal) amounts to £3.1 billion, while the loss to the economy is £2.7 billion. This amounts to over £5.7 billion a year. The costs can be broken down as follows:

■ **Criminal Justice System:** The cost of domestic violence to the criminal justice system (CJS) is around £1 billion a year. This is nearly one-quarter of the CJS budget for violent crime. The largest single component is that of the police. Other components include: prosecution, courts, probation, prison, and legal aid.

■ **Health Care:** The cost to the NHS for physical injuries is around £1.2 billion a year. This includes GPs and hospitals. Physical injuries account for most of the NHS costs, but there is an important element of mental health care, estimated at an additional £176 million.

■ **Social Services:** The annual cost is nearly £.25 billion. This is overwhelmingly for children rather than for adults, especially those caught up in the co-occurrence of domestic violence and child abuse.

■ **Housing:** Expenditure on emergency housing includes costs to Local Housing Authorities and Housing Associations for housing those homeless because of domestic violence; housing benefit for such emergency housing; and, importantly, refuges. This amounts to £.16 billion a year.

■ **Civil Legal:** Civil legal services cost over £.3 billion, about half of which is borne by legal aid and half by the individual. This includes both specialist legal actions such as injunctions to restrain or expel a violent partner, as well as actions consequent on the disentangling of marriages and relationships such as divorce and child custody.

■ **Economic Output:** Lost economic output accounts for around £2.7 billion a year. This is the cost of time off work due to injuries. It is estimated that around half of the costs of such sickness absences is borne by the employer and half by the individual in lost wages. An additional element is the human and emotional cost. Domestic violence leads to pain and suffering that is not counted in the cost of services. This amounts to over £17 billion a year. Including all costs, the total cost of domestic violence for the state, employers and victims is estimated at around £23 billion.

■ The above information is from the DTI's Women and Equality Unit website which can be found at www.womenandequalityunit.gov.uk

The cycle of abuse

Information from Medicine Hat College, Canada

People may not understand why you stay in the abusive situation. There are many reasons why. You may not want to admit to anyone that your partner is hurting you. The abuser may be someone you love. He may support the family or be the father of your children.

Certain situations may trigger the abuse. You may tend to blame yourself... 'If only I had not burned the supper. If only I had not bought a dress with a short hemline.

If only ...'

Why does he blame me?

The abuser may blame you too. He may think you caused his jealousy or anger. Abusers usually blame some-body else for their acts. Often they drink and blame their abuse on alcohol. They may feel pressured at work and think they can take it out on women. They may believe that women are not equal to men and that men have the right to discipline you. They almost always have an excuse for their actions.

Why does it happen again and again?

Sometimes he feels bad. He says he is sorry and you accept. You believe things will change. Life seems to get better. Tension builds. The next time it happens, the abuse seems worse. Frightened and angry, you leave. Again, he apologises and you go back. Almost all abused women go back at least once.

When he is not beating you, he may be very loving and caring. But each time you return the abuse may get worse. It happens more often. You may feel trapped and alone.

Am I the only woman going through this?

You may feel you are the only person in the world who is beaten or humiliated by your partner. You may be too afraid or too ashamed to even tell your friends or get help.

You may be especially afraid if you have tried to leave before. Your fear gives him the power to control you.

They almost always have an excuse.

You have three choices:
1. Accept the relationship and live with it.
2. Stay in the relationship and try to make changes.
3. Leave the relationship and get on with life.

Choice #1: Accept the relationship

You may stay in an abusive relation-ship. Out of love or fear, money concerns or other reasons, you give in to your partner. You learn to live with the abusive relationship.

What should I be prepared for?
Living with abuse is a dangerous choice. If you choose to stay, there are a few things that you should know:

- Ignoring his insults or hoping that things will get better some day does not work. Chances are, things will get worse.
- Many women living in abusive relationships end up being killed, committing suicide or killing their partner.
- If you stay in an abusive relation-ship, your children may suffer.
- If you stay, please remember: you never deserve to be beaten or abused.

Most abuse is a crime. No one has the legal right to hurt you.

What about the children?
Children living in abusive situations may be emotionally or physically abused themselves.

Children who see their father abuse their mother are often anxious and confused. They may even lose respect for their mother.

Boys often become aggressive while girls become withdrawn. Later on in life, girls may find themselves in abusive situations and boys may grow into abusive men.

What are my responsibilities?
Your children may not be victims of abuse themselves, but you must keep them safe. If you do not take steps to protect your children from an abusive situation, the government (Child Protection Services) can take them from your custody and put them in protective care.

Choice #2: Change the relationship

You may decide to stay with your partner and try to make changes. Keep the following in mind.

Can I change him?
Just because he keeps saying 'sorry' and promising he will change, does not mean he will. When you go back to him he has no more reason to change. Some men make this promise just to keep their partners.

How will I know if he is ready to change?
He must do three things before change is possible:
- He must admit that the way he treats you is wrong.
- He must decide that he needs help.

- He must be willing to go for counselling for a long time to unlearn his behaviour.

Will I or my children need counselling?

Yes. You will need to learn to live without abuse and how to respect yourself. Joining a support group with other women who have been abused may help you to find the strength to live your own life. Your children will need help and counselling to see that abuse is the wrong way to solve problems.

What if nothing changes?

Be prepared. Change will not happen overnight. It takes a long time. Remember, the situation might even become abusive again. You should be prepared for this possibility. Know your rights and plan an escape route.

Choice #3: Leave!

You have the right to live a life free of abuse. You can decide to be free of the abuse by getting out of the relationship and getting on with your life. When you do this, you will probably need legal advice.

What steps can I take when I'm ready to leave?

If you are thinking about leaving your abusive partner, you should try to set up an escape plan.
- Make sure you have important documents set aside
- Save money in secret if you can
- Find a safe place to go: friends, shelter, family
- Keep extra keys and clothes with friends
- Secure transportation
- Work out a signal system with a friend
- Go when he is gone
- Don't tell him you are leaving
- Create an excuse to slip away.

Should I take any papers or documents with me?

Even before you are ready to leave, try to collect and copy the following documents and keep them in a safe place.
- Driver's licence/Registration
- Credit cards and bank card
- Personal identification (including picture ID)
- Birth certificate
- Immunisation card for the children
- Custody order
- Personal cheque book
- Last banking statement
- Mortgage papers

Should I plan to take any personal items with me?

When leaving an abusive situation you should try to take personal items such as:
- Prescribed medication
- Personal hygiene products
- Glasses/contact lenses
- Money (if possible)
- Clothing (nightwear, underwear)
- Heirlooms, jewellery
- Photo albums (pictures that you want to keep)
- Craft, needle work, hobby work
- Children's items such as soothers/bottles, clothing, special blanket and/or toy.

You have the right to live a life free of abuse.

■ The above information is from the Women's Rights section of the Medicine Hat College website, a resource for women who are being abused by their partner. Visit www.mhc.ab.ca/programs/con_studies/womens_rights for more.
© Medicine Hat College

Older women suffer domestic violence in silence

Information from Help the Aged

Older women who experience domestic violence are forced to suffer in silence says a new report by Help the Aged and Hact.

They are being let down by professionals, service providers and ignored by policy makers because of an inherent belief that domestic violence stops at 60.

Kate Jopling, Public Affairs Officer for Help the Aged, said: 'Society has created a huge wall of ignorance around the issue of domestic violence for older women.

'Older women have grown up in a culture when domestic violence was not even considered a crime. Therefore they are less likely to believe themselves a victim, let alone report such violence.

'This is coupled with stereotypical views that older women do not have intimate relationships, and that older men are rarely a serious threat.'

The report claims that marks of physical injury are often attributed to falls and if an older women discloses incidences of such violence it can be put down to confusion or dementia.

In tackling the issues faced by women over 60 the report recommends:
- Research to identify the scope of the problem;
- Specific services designed to meet the needs of older women;
- Closer working relationship between workers in adult protection and the domestic violence field;
- Training and support for professionals and healthcare workers to help identify and support older women.

A 24-hour national domestic violence helpline is available on freephone 0808 2000 247. To order a copy of the report, *Older Women and Domestic Violence*, priced £8, please contact us at the following address: publications@helptheaged.org.uk

■ The above information is from Help the Aged's website which can be found at www.helptheaged.org.uk
© Help the Aged 2004

Fighting back

Domestic abuse represents up to a quarter of violent crime in UK cities. Tina Orr Munro visits the Women's Safety Unit in Cardiff where securing more convictions is key to tackling the problem

Hilary Clode's husband subjected her to 25 years of physical and mental abuse, so when she decided to take him to court for assault he never expected her to go through with it. 'When I walked into that court room, I could tell by the look of shock on his face he didn't think I would show up,' says the 50-year-old mother of four.

Hilary's husband, a former police officer, was right to assume she would not turn up. Domestic violence in most towns and cities represents 25% of violent crime by volume, but few men are prosecuted because women often fail to pursue their complaint.

Hilary's case was heard by Cardiff's Special Domestic Violence Court, which is one of five such courts across the country that have been set up to secure more convictions. Jan Pickles, manager of the city's Women's Safety Unit, helped develop the court after it became clear the criminal justice system was failing women like Hilary. 'The victim wasn't even in the process. The perpetrator would go along to the courts and say they had got back together and the courts would accept their word. Agencies such as the police also felt let down.

By Tina Orr Munro

They worked to get the case to court only to watch the perpetrator get off,' she says.

Although the unit's primary concern is the woman's personal safety, it recognises the importance of getting abusers convicted as a way of reducing domestic violence. 'Convictions are effective. It is important to get one, but it is not the only reason. If the perpetrator has lots of previous convictions, it may not make any difference,' says Pickles.

'The aim is to increase her safety and not put her through a stressful situation if it is not going to make life better for her. Many don't want to go to court because they don't want the perpetrator to get a custodial sentence. All we can do is give risk information. Up until then they have been making decisions in a vacuum, they have normalised an abnormal situation.'

For women who proceed with a prosecution, the unit allocates an advocate to support them throughout the process. Advocates include a seconded police officer and a practising magistrate with years of experience of the criminal justice system. Their role is to keep women informed of their case's progress, liaise with the courts and coordinate all the agencies involved. Advocates also accompany the women to the pre-trial hearing, which was identified by the unit as where many cases are discontinued.

Domestic violence in most towns and cities represents 25% of violent crime by volume, but few men are prosecuted because women often fail to pursue their complaint

'The pre-trial review is where deals were being done, cases were being dropped and bail conditions were being altered because the perpetrator said they had got back together, or if the victim turned up they said under duress that they didn't want to proceed,' says Pickles.

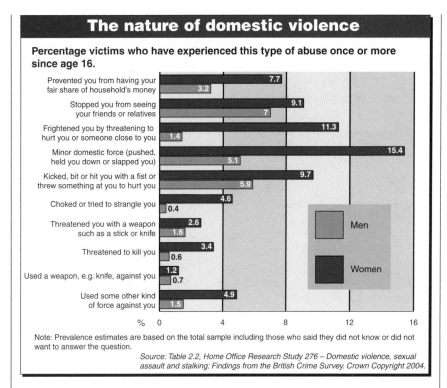

The nature of domestic violence

Percentage victims who have experienced this type of abuse once or more since age 16.

Type of abuse	Men	Women
Prevented you from having your fair share of household's money	3.2	7.7
Stopped you from seeing your friends or relatives	7	9.1
Frightened you by threatening to hurt you or someone close to you	1.4	11.3
Minor domestic force (pushed, held you down or slapped you)	5.1	15.4
Kicked, bit or hit you with a fist or threw something at you to hurt you	5.9	9.7
Choked or tried to strangle you	0.4	4.6
Threatened you with a weapon such as a stick or knife	1.6	2.6
Threatened to kill you	0.6	3.4
Used a weapon, e.g. knife, against you	0.7	1.2
Used some other kind of force against you	1.5	4.9

% 0   4   8   12   16

Note: Prevalence estimates are based on the total sample including those who said they did not know or did not want to answer the question.

Source: Table 2.2, Home Office Research Study 276 – Domestic violence, sexual assault and stalking: Findings from the British Crime Survey. Crown Copyright 2004.

After the pre-trial review, the cases are then flagged to the courts and fast-tracked through the system. In Cardiff, cases are heard within six weeks of the review as opposed to 16 weeks under the old regime. That time could be reduced further, says Pickles, but she believes it is important for women to have the opportunity to understand the process and reflect on what has happened to them. If the case moves to the crown court, the unit tries to ensure it is heard early in the week, alongside other serious crimes.

Better training for those who work in the criminal justice system has also been key to improving the service. Some 80 magistrates, 27 prosecutors and 200 defence lawyers have received awareness training, including introducing the idea that children are often the secondary victims in domestic violence cases. Other improvements include encouraging referrals to the unit not just from the usual quarters, such as the police, but also from the A&E department of Cardiff's University Hospital, and even defence lawyers.

A special form to identify women who are most at risk was introduced in December 2002 for police officers to fill out when attending domestic violence incidents. The form was developed with the Domestic Violence Prevention Service of the NSPCC and is based on a review of 47 domestic homicides. A score of more than six out of the 15 risk indicators means the woman is in danger and her case is examined at a Marac – multi-agency risk assessment conference – which is held every month and attended by representatives from 16 agencies including the police, probation, health, housing and the NSPCC.

The number of victims who refuse to press charges after reporting an incident has steadily reduced, from 59% before the unit opened to 2% by October 2004

By sharing information and their expertise, the agencies decide how to reduce further harm to the victim. 'It used to take us three hours to discuss just one case. We now review 20 to 30 cases in that time,' says Pickles.

The Women's Safety Unit, funded by the Welsh assembly and opened in November 2001, has so far helped over 7,000 women and their children. In that time, repeat victimisation has fallen from 30% to 15% in Cardiff. Pickles is hopeful this can be further reduced. 'We could get it down to 4% or 5% if we micromanage cases and make sure we have the referrals and see what is being done.'

The number of victims who refuse to press charges after reporting an incident has steadily reduced, from 59% before the unit opened to 2% by October 2004. Cardiff's success has been replicated in the four other domestic violence courts in Wolverhampton, west London, Leeds, and Derby.

A 2004 study by the Crown Prosecution Service and Department for Constitutional Affairs (DCA), as part of a CPS two-year project on domestic violence, found that the courts have had a positive effect and recommended that they be extended to cover other areas. Last month the DCA announced plans to set up more courts.

In Hilary's case, her appearance at court prompted her husband to change his plea from self-defence to guilty. He was given a conditional discharge. They are now divorced and she is rebuilding her life. Last month she was employed by the unit as an administrative assistant. She also runs a survivors' forum and has completed a counselling diploma.

'I could never had done without the support of the unit. They were there every step of the way,' she says. 'Now I give support to others. I believe we are coming into an era where domestic abuse isn't hush-hush any more. There is no need for women to feel ashamed about what has happened to them.'

© *Guardian Newspapers Limited 2005*

Why do women stay with violent men?

Information from Justice for Women

There are many reasons why women stay with violent partners, and each case is unique and should be viewed individually. However, there are some underlying beliefs that make women stay. There is the overall stigma and embarrassment attached to these relationships with common ignorant beliefs such as she must have deserved it, she must like it or she would leave, or it is a private matter between husband and wife. The most effective form of abuse is thought to be emotional, which is why men use not only physical violence but a combination of mental, verbal, economic and sexual abuse to control women. They gradually wear the woman down, creating total fear and dependence and a lack of self-belief and confidence in themselves and anyone else around them. Outwardly the couple may appear happy and 'normal', as these men are often charming and deceptive, so there would be the issue of disbelief and scandal.

It is extremely difficult for someone who has not experienced this kind of treatment to understand how it affects women and why they stay, but there are some common factors that we will cover here. Firstly the woman has memories of a loving partner and believes that he will change and become the person she once knew. He makes excuses for his violence that the woman comes to believe, such as it is due to stress or that it is her fault he behaves this way and she shouldn't have done this or that to provoke him. Also there is the notion of better

the devil you know, or the children love him and would miss him, or refuse to leave.

Men have several methods of controlling women and preventing them from talking about what is happening or seeking help. Children are regularly used to ensure women stay by either threats of violence and abuse towards them or by women having the misled belief that their children will be taken from them by agencies such as social services if they make the violence known. Whilst it is true that social services would wish to remove the children from that environment, they would prefer to keep the mother and children together, reducing the risk of further stress to either party. We must remember that in over 90% of cases of domestic violence the

children are present or in a room next door and there are very strong links between domestic violence and child abuse (Messages From Research, 1995).

Men frequently control and lessen the woman's freedom by running all economic aspects of the relationship, i.e. running the home, shopping etc., creating financial dependence. If the woman were given an allowance, she would have to account for every penny spent, preventing the opportunity to save enough money to attempt to leave. It also creates a fear of leaving as it presents huge problems when thinking of feeding and housing herself or her children and often would mean leaving all or most of their possessions. Many women do not know their rights or what help is available to them, so do not have the know-how to leave immediately. This in turn creates an isolation, which is compounded by the abuser when he makes threats, particularly to other family members and friends, which are effective because the woman knows exactly what he is capable of. This results in her belief that she cannot turn to them to provide a safe place to stay for fear of placing them in great danger.

In addition, consideration must be given to those women who cannot or have not been allowed to learn the English language or who have religious or cultural reasons for staying in a violent relationship. They may believe that the violence is 'normal', or believe that to leave would bring dishonour to the family, consequently resulting in the woman being ostracised, not

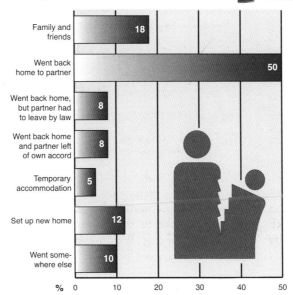

Fleeing domestic violence

Destination of domestic violence victims after initial flight, female, in last year.
Unweighted N = 127.

- Family and friends: 18
- Went back home to partner: 50
- Went back home, but partner had to leave by law: 8
- Went back home and partner left of own accord: 8
- Temporary accommodation: 5
- Set up new home: 12
- Went somewhere else: 10

% 0 10 20 30 40 50

Notes:
1. Source 2001 BCS.
2. Multiple reponses were allowed, therefore percentages will not sum to 100.
3. Excludes 'don't know' and 'don't want to answer' responses.

Source: Table 4.5, Home Office Research Study 276 – Domestic violence, sexual assault and stalking: Findings from the British Crime Survey. Crown Copyright 2004.

only by family but by her community as well. This may also mean that the woman would lose her immigration status, and would have to leave or fight to stay, which of course would mean she had no recourse to public funds and could not work, so would struggle to support herself, let alone a family. Also, if there are language barriers, she hasn't been told what her rights are and what agencies could help her; in fact the abuser usually instils a fear of professional services in the woman.

Changes in attitude around domestic violence are slow, and there are still difficulties within the judiciary and police systems, which creates a fear of reporting this crime and a disbelief in justice being served. The following quotes are extreme examples of these negative attitudes:

- Summing up in a rape trial, Judge Raymond Dodd said: 'When women say no, they don't always mean no. Men can't turn their emotions on and off like a tap as some women do.'

- Before releasing on probation a man who admitted repeated sexual assaults on his 12-year-old stepdaughter, Judge Sir Harold Cassel said: 'A pregnant wife's

lack of sexual appetite leads to considerable problems for healthy young husbands.'

It is important to note there are many reasons why a woman stays with a violent man and this explanation is not exhaustive, it merely gives a snapshot of the more common reasons.

■ Information from Justice for Women – please see www.jfw.org.uk

Violence people like to ignore

Domestic violence against men is a subject society seems happy to ignore. Reporter Michelle Frame spoke to one male victim who is determined to lift this wall of silence. . .

Imagine being beaten repeatedly by the person you love most. Imagine the terror of being threatened with a knife and feeling so scared you cannot even make a drink without fearing reprisals.

Now imagine no-one believes you. This is George Rolph's true story.

As a male victim of domestic violence, he is only too aware of the stigma faced by battered husbands.

In 1996 the 50-year-old, of Capstone Road, Downham, was ecstatic after meeting a woman he got on well with, little knowing she would eventually make him suicidal.

He said: 'We got on really, really well but a couple of months later she started to get violent.

'I didn't even dare make a cup of tea and was kept in a state of constant anxiety.'

Gradually the woman's behaviour became worse but, like many male perpetrators, George's partner seemed unable to accept she was doing anything wrong.

He said: 'I spent all morning making a shelf but because I didn't use the piece of wood she had got she hit me with it.

'She cracked my head open and then, as I lay on the floor, she smacked the wardrobe door in my face.

'My shirt had turned red because I was bleeding but she just asked me what I wanted for dinner as if nothing had happened.'

However, George feels it is the emotional abuse which can cause the most problems.

He said: 'The experiences most of us go through are the drip, drip, drip kind which wear away at our self-esteem, our confidence, our ability to fight back. Those wounds often do not heal.'

The prejudice faced by male victims is something George, a former motorcycle courier, has dedicated his life to fighting.

Determined to turn around his experiences, including a second violent relationship, he set up the support organisation Man2Man and was shocked when he received more than 1,000 emails.

His message to society seems simple: a victim is a victim regardless of race or gender.

In his quest to help male victims George has beaten down many doors but he feels those of Lewisham Council are yet to fall.

After making a presentation last year and becoming a member of Lewisham's Domestic Violence Forum, George was hoping for funding to distribute leaflets and train helpline operators.

He believes his plea fell on deaf ears but a spokesman for the council denied it did not take the issue seriously.

The spokesman said: 'The council aims to support all groups and communities including men. The same services as there are for women apply for men with the exception of a refuge.'

■ Courtesy of News Shopper – please see www.newsshopper.co.uk

Hidden victims

A survey of 100 male victims of domestic violence has found general bias against them, with fathers particularly affected

A recently published report of research by Dewar Research summarises the main findings of the experiences reported by 100 male victims of domestic violence (49 from England and Wales, and 51 from Ireland) to a survey conducted in 2001.

The responses generally corroborate the experiences of male victims gleaned from the few other previous detailed surveys, such as the Home Office Research Study 191 (published in January 1999, but based on fieldwork in 1995), and the *Dispatches* programme survey in 1998, also specifically of male victims, the results of this latter survey being summarised in a broadcast by Channel 4 on 7th January 1999. They also reflect the findings of academic studies published both in this country and abroad. Each of the surveys reported complaints by many male victims of the general bias against them in the responses they had received from the police, prosecution service, the courts, and other agencies.

35% of male victims reported that the police had totally ignored what they had to say

---

Responses to the Dewar Research 2001 Survey appear to support such complaints. For English and Welsh male victims, they found:

- 50% were threatened with a weapon;
- 33% were kicked in the genitals;
- 16% were burnt or scalded;
- 40% received severe bruising to the body;
- 75% were assaulted once a month or more frequently;
- over two-thirds were assaulted more than 10 times;
- 35% reported that the police had totally ignored what they had to say;
- 47% reported that they had been threatened with arrest despite being the victim;
- 21% said that they had been arrested despite being the victim;
- only 3% reported that the violent female partner had been arrested;
- female assailants called the police nearly as often as the male victim (53% of occasions compared to 59%);
- of the few female assailants arrested and subsequently charged, not one was convicted, despite the serious injuries some of the male victims had suffered.

The results reinforce previous findings of a general underlying bias and prejudice against male victims in domestic violence practice and procedures by both police and the prosecution service. This replicates exactly similar findings both in North America and Australia.

Father victims appear to be particularly disadvantaged by the bias.

The police, prosecution service, and the courts appear reluctant to take any action against the violent or abusive mothers. The result is that many father victims have no choice but to remain silent since reporting the violence against them appears usually to result in them, rather than the violent mother, being removed from the home and subsequently losing meaningful contact with their children. It appears that problems over contact with their children are a particular feature of the experience of male victims once relationships break down (Reference: Male Domestic Viol-ence Victims Survey 2001 – Main Findings. Dewar Research, October 2004.)

Full details of the 2001 Survey results, and other information on domestic violence and male victim-isation, can be found on the Dewar Research website which can be found at www.dewar4research.org

Background information

Despite the ever-increasing evidence of male victimisation in intimate relationships, as shown by now well over one hundred gender-neutral studies, little information exists in the public domain about the particular plight of male victims. This is in contrast to that of female victims, for which there is now a considerable amount of information.

The Dewar Research 2001 Survey of 100 male victims was designed to redress that imbalance in some small way.

Dewar Research is a small voluntary private initiative formed in 1996 to collate information available in the public domain in order to encourage more informed debate of social issues. As such, it calls on professional and academic expertise as required.

For the purpose of the 2001 Survey, Dewar Research collaborated with Dr Malcolm George FRSA, a neuroscientist, who has published widely in academic journals on the issue of domestic violence and related aspects, including the historical context of male victimisation. His latest paper *Invisible Touch* was published in 2003 in the journal *Aggression and Violent Behaviour*.

The co-author and research coordinator for Dewar Research, David Yarwood, is a chartered civil engineer who has published several studies relating to the issue of domestic violence on behalf of Dewar Research.

- Information reprinted with kind permission from Mankind – for more information please visit their website at www.mankind.org.uk or see page 41 for address details.

© Mankind 2005

Women say they'd walk . . . ◆ ◆ ◆

. . . but few do. New domestic violence statistics show scale of living in fear

New research out today (3 September 2004) reveals that almost 10 million British women claim they'd leave immediately if a partner struck them.

When questioned about how they'd react if physically assaulted for the first time by a current or future partner, 41 per cent of female adults say they'd leave straight away.

Yet the shocking reality is that a woman suffering domestic violence will be beaten an average of 35 times before finally calling the police.

The study by The Body Shop – as it launches its 'Donate a Phone, Save a Life' campaign with national domestic violence charity Women's Aid to provide a lifeline to vulnerable women – reveals the alarming inconsistency between how women think they'd behave if abused by their partner and the reality.

Whilst 20 per cent of women admit they have lived, or do currently live in fear of violence happening, more than half (52 per cent) told researchers for The Body Shop they'd be too embarrassed and ashamed to tell their friends. Even more (59 per cent) would stay tight-lipped with family.

The personal alarm scheme, the first of its kind in the UK for domestic violence victims, will be rolled out initially in Birmingham and then in London, Norwich, Bristol and Glasgow over the next six months.

The 'Donate a Phone, Save a Life' campaign urges people across the UK to donate old or unwanted mobile phones. These phones will be used to generate mobile personal alarms – with direct dial to 999 at the touch of any button – and distributed to at-risk women.

Freepost envelopes to donate the handsets are available to pick up at over 300 stores of The Body Shop across the UK.

Launching the partnership at a women's support centre in south London, Dame Anita Roddick, founder of The Body Shop, said she

hopes this new campaign will not only provide a much needed lifeline for vulnerable women, but empower everyone to act and help stop violence in the home.

She said: 'Leaving a violent relationship isn't as easy as you may think. In fact, our research shows that three in five women would be too ashamed to even tell their own mother that they were being abused by their partner.

'A woman is often at her most vulnerable when planning to leave, or having just left a violent relationship. That's why The Body Shop is launching this personal alarm scheme, providing women with a lifeline at a time when they need it most.

'I personally urge everyone to rally behind this campaign and search out old mobile phones that may be hanging around at home and in the workplace, and donate them to help bring this amazing initiative to life.'

Nicola Harwin CBE, Director of national domestic violence charity Women's Aid, said: 'Millions of women live with the fear of violence every day and yet many will tell no one.

'Instead, they will suffer in silence because they don't know where to turn or are too afraid or ashamed to reveal their abuse – we hope that this new and innovative campaign with The Body Shop will help increase protection for women at risk by providing them with a direct route to the police.'

The 'Donate a Phone, Save a Life' campaign aims to provide a much-needed solution to the dangers faced by many female victims of domestic violence. Mobiles phones collected

by The Body Shop – who estimate there could be as many as 17 million mobile handsets unused across the UK – will either be converted into a personal alarm by Fonesforsafety or recycled to raise funds to support the scheme.

Domestic violence survivor Bryony, who was abused by her husband for more than three years before fleeing, applauded the new mobile personal alarm scheme.

Bryony said: 'I suffered in silence for a long time, hiding my secret from family and friends for years before finding the strength to leave. Having a mobile personal alarm would have made a real difference and potentially given me the confidence to leave sooner. I ask everyone to donate their old mobiles to support this much needed initiative and help women and children everywhere.'

Assistant Chief Constable Jim Gamble, Association of Chief Police Officers (ACPO) Lead for Domestic Violence and Harassment, added: 'The police are concerned with holding perpetrators to account and protecting victims of this crime. I fully support the personal alarm scheme as it will aid victim protection by allowing them to have safer and more direct access to the police. I would encourage everyone with a spare mobile phone to donate it to The Body Shop. You can make a difference, you can help victims of domestic violence and perhaps even save a life.'

■ Women's Aid is the national domestic violence charity which co-ordinates and supports an England-wide network of over 300 local projects, providing over 500 refuges, helplines, outreach services and advice centres.

Reproduced with kind permission from Women's Aid – please visit www.womensaid.org.uk

© The Women's Aid Federation of England 2004 (www.womensaid.org.uk)

Domestic violence

Information taken from a ChildLine information sheet

'My parents argue a lot. Last night I came home, Dad was hitting Mum. It's really upset me. When I tried to help, Dad told me to go away.' Amy, 12

What is domestic violence?

Domestic violence is aggression or violence that happens in the home when a grown-up attacks or threatens another adult in the family. In most cases, the violence is carried out by a man against a woman, although not always.

Domestic violence can happen in any family and in all kinds of homes. In half of the cases of violence between adults, children get hurt too. Even when children do not see the violence happening, they often hear it. Children are often in the same or next room when the violence is going on. This can be extremely distressing and disturbing for them.

Domestic violence can mean lots of different things. These include:

- physical abuse – hurting someone by hitting, pushing or kicking
- sexual abuse – forcing or encouraging someone to take part in sexual behaviour in any way that makes them uncomfortable (see ChildLine's website for their information sheet on Child Abuse)
- emotional abuse – saying things on purpose to frighten the other person or putting them down to make them feel bad. For example, constantly saying that someone is stupid or ugly
- controlling behaviour – preventing someone by force from acting freely. This can include keeping them from seeing relatives and friends, not letting them have a job or not letting them spend money.

The facts of domestic violence

Grown-ups and children should feel safe and secure in their homes. When domestic violence happens, home becomes a frightening, unsafe place to live. Domestic violence is wrong and families do not have to put up with it.

- More than half a million incidents (635,000) of domestic violence are reported in England and Wales each year. Most victims are women, but domestic violence can happen to men too.
- In nine out of ten cases, children are in the same or next room when the violence is going on.
- In five out of ten cases when there is violence between adults, children get hurt too.
- One in four women experience domestic violence sometime in

their lives. Between six per cent and ten per cent of women experience domestic violence in any one year.

- Almost 2,000 children a year contact ChildLine due to problems of domestic violence.

Domestic violence – how it affects children and young people

Physical abuse

'Dad hits me and Mum most days. He's always hit us. He doesn't work and drinks all day. I want it to stop. I'm so unhappy. Dad says he will kill us if we leave.' Gerry, 12

Above all, children living in a home where there is domestic violence are at risk of being hurt themselves. This may be because the violent person in the family hurts them on purpose. Sometimes, though, children and young people get injured by accident when they try to help the person being attacked.

Emotional abuse

'Me and my sister are scared. Our parents fight a lot and we fear they might split up. They fight when we're upstairs. They don't think we know what's going on, but we do.' Mandy, 9

Children and young people can be deeply upset and disturbed by domestic violence in their family, even if they are not physically hurt themselves. They may hear the fighting downstairs or even be in the same room when it is happening.

If other members of the family pretend nothing is wrong, it can make children feel worse about what is going on.

Domestic violence can also force children and young people to take sides and choose between their parents, even though they don't want to. Mum and dad are the two people children love most in the world. Seeing one hurt the other is extremely upsetting.

Neglect

'Mum's always miserable. She never asks me how I am. She just sits in front of the telly all day. I could be dead for all she cares.'
Wayne, 13

Many mothers continue to provide love and support when they are suffering domestic violence. But when a woman is beaten or constantly criticised, it can be difficult for her to be happy and for her to look after herself and her children. As a result, children living in homes where there is domestic violence can feel neglected and left to look after themselves. They can feel that no one takes an interest in them and that no one cares.

They may have to do household chores for themselves like cooking, washing clothes, and food shopping.

Fear and loss of confidence

'I'm churned up inside. I'm so confused. When I tried to talk to my mum about being hurt, she told me not to be stupid and denied that anything was wrong. I want to leave home, but don't want to leave Mum alone. I'm drinking a lot.'
John, 18

Children and young people react in different ways to being brought up in a home with a violent partner. Most children are disturbed and upset by domestic violence. Some become angry and blame one or other of the adults involved. Others copy the violence and bully or hurt others.

Often, children and young people lose confidence. They feel guilty, ashamed, afraid, angry or embarrassed about what's happening in their home. They often try to cover up and do not tell people what's happening. It is the family 'secret'.

Domestic violence can make life very confusing for young people. They may feel that they have to look after the parent who is being hurt, even if it means putting themselves in danger. Also children and young people may feel so stressed that they can't concentrate on their school work or sleep well at night.

When there is domestic violence in the home, small children and babies may not understand what is going on, but they often display signs that they are unhappy and feeling insecure. They may be more demanding and get upset over little things. They may need more attention and cuddles. Children that don't wet the bed may start doing so, which can make them feel embarrassed or stupid.

Is it my fault?

'Dad sometimes hits Mum when he's angry. I think it might be my fault because I can never get things right with my dad.' Natalie, 14

If there is domestic violence in your home, you must always remember that it is not your fault. It is only the fault of the person who is violent. Do not feel ashamed or think you could have stopped the violence or nasty behaviour if you had behaved differently. The chances are that the person being violent would have done what they did anyway. Do not blame yourself.

How can I stop the violence?

The only person who can stop the violence is the person who is doing it. If there is violence at home, though, you can get help. There are things you can do to keep yourself, your brothers and sisters and your mum safe.

Here are some suggestions:

- keep yourself safe. Find a safe place – like a bedroom – where you can hide until the violence is over
- only help your mother (or whoever is being hurt) if it means you will not place yourself at risk
- talk to someone you like and trust, such as a teacher, a friend or your social worker (if you have one) about what's happening at home. They will listen to your problems and you can talk about what to do next. At ChildLine we know that friends can give a lot of help and support if you are worried about something
- call the police on 999 (Minicom 0800 112 999)
- try to get your mum to seek help. Show her the phone numbers at the end of this article
- call ChildLine on 0800 1111 or one of the helplines in this article. Children living with domestic violence often tell ChildLine that they feel alone and that no one listens to them. Talking to a counsellor at ChildLine who listens and takes your problems seriously can help you feel less lonely. It can also give you the confidence to seek help if you want. At ChildLine, children talk at their

own pace. We never force you to tell us anything. ChildLine is the free and confidential counselling service for any child or young person with any problem and is available 24 hours a day, every day.

What is a refuge?

'Mum and I are in a refuge because Dad hits Mum. He hit her so bad she had to go to hospital. I now go to a new school. I can't keep in touch with old friends in case they tell Dad where I am.' Terry, 9

Refuges are houses in normal streets like other homes, but their addresses are only known by the people who live in them.

Women and children can go and live in one of these safe houses – or refuges – to get away from violence. Women and their children can stay at a refuge for any length of time – from one night to a year – until they can return home safely or move somewhere new.

Leaving home can give families a chance to have a new life without the violence. But it can bring some changes that are unsettling. Children and young people may be concerned that they won't be able to keep in touch with family members or old friends, or that they will have to go to a different school.

Groups like Women's Aid and Refuge (see *Further information and advice*) can tell you or your mum about refuges in your area.

Sometimes the police can force the violent person to leave the family home, so that the rest of the family can stay there. Some families get support from social services if they are having problems.

I want the violence to stop, but I don't want Mum and Dad to split up. What can I do?

All children are troubled by domestic violence, but they may still love the person who is being violent. They worry that if they tell someone what is happening or seek help, then their parents will split up.

Some children and young people get very frustrated with the victim for being unable to stop the abuse.

Or they may be afraid that they won't be able to escape the violence, even if they do leave the family home.

Parents need to sort out their problems for the violence to stop. Let them know how much it hurts you when they fight. They may not know how upset you are or even realise you know the violence is happening.

Why does Mum stay at home?

'Why doesn't Mum leave her boyfriend? She's not happy. When I asked her, she said I'm too young to understand.' Mark, 14

Many women do leave the person hurting them, but it takes a lot of courage. Lots of families live with abuse for many months or even years.

Lots of families live with abuse for many months or even years

---

Women stay with abusive partners for many reasons. They may be too scared to leave. They may not have any money or anywhere to go. They may worry about taking their children out of school and moving to a new area. They may be so worn down by all that's happened and not have the strength to go. Children and young people often do not understand this. As they get older, their confusion may change into anger and disgust.

You can help by trying to get your mum to call one of the numbers in this article.

What is the law?

Domestic violence is a crime. Victims are protected by the law. The Government may also bring in new laws to protect families from violence. Contact one of the following organisations to find out more.

Further information and advice

- **Women's Aid Federation of England**
  England's national charity for women and children experiencing physical, sexual or emotional abuse in their homes. 24-hour domestic violence helpline.

Tel: 08457 023 468
www.womensaid.org.uk
- **Scottish Women's Aid**
  Tel: 0131 475 2372
  www.scottishwomensaid.co.uk
- **Welsh Women's Aid**
  Tel: 029 20390874
- **Northern Ireland Women's Aid Federation**
  Tel: 02890 331818
  www.niwaf.org
- **Parentline Plus**
  UK-wide helpline for anyone caring for children and young people.
  Tel: 0808 800 2222
  Textphone: 0800 783 6783
  www.parentlineplus.org.uk
- **Refuge**
  24-hour UK-wide domestic violence crisis line.
  Tel: 08705 995 443
- **Kiran**
  Asian Women's Aid – Advice, support, refuge and outreach help for Asian women and children.
  Tel: 020 8558 1986
- **Southall Black Sisters**
  Information and advice for black and Asian women on domestic violence and related issues.
  Tel: 020 8571 9595
- **Police**
  In an emergency call 999, or Textphone 0800 112 999
- **NSPCC**
  Child protection helpline for anyone in England, Wales or Northern Ireland concerned about the safety of a child. Asian language service also available.
  Tel: 0808 800 5000
  Textphone: 0800 056 0566
  www.nspcc.org.uk
- **Everyman Project**
  Counselling, support and advice for men who are violent or concerned about their violence, and anyone affected by that violence.
  Tel: 020 7737 6747
- **Home Office**
  'Loves Me Not' – leaflet on domestic violence
  www.homeoffice.gov.uk

- Information reprinted with kind permission from ChildLine – visit www.childline.org.uk for more, or see page 41 for address details.
  © *ChildLine*

Why does domestic violence happen?

Information from www.thehideout.org.uk

I've heard it happens more to women

Most of the time domestic violence happens between men and women, when men abuse women; but it can happen to men, too. When you look at the roles of men and women in history it can help you to understand why it happens more to women.

150 years ago in the UK it was still legal for a man to beat his wife, as long as the stick was no thicker than his thumb. Historically, women had very few legal rights: they couldn't own property or divorce their husbands; they could only work in certain jobs and were paid much less than men. In many societies, it's been the role of women to mind the home, cook, clean and care for the children and for their husband. Traditionally, it's been the man's role to work and earn the money for the family. Men made the rules and women and children had to follow them. A man had the right to beat his wife and children if he felt they deserved it.

In the UK, a lot has changed since then – things are much better now! In the last century women have fought hard to win more rights, such as the right to vote, the right to study and to work. Women now have careers and men and women share

THE HIDEOUT

www.thehideout.org.uk

until children are safe

the responsibilities of taking care of the home and children.

Men and women should be treated as equals, but this is still not always the case. Many societies and cultures still believe that men are stronger and more powerful than women and this makes some people think that violence between men and women is okay – but it's not! Men and women are still working hard today to change this way of thinking and to stop domestic violence from happening.

No excuses

There is never an excuse for domestic violence. All types of abuse are wrong and the victim is never to blame. Children and young people are also never to blame for domestic violence that happens between adults. It is not your fault – even if the argument is about you!

Domestic violence is about power and control. The abuser feels powerful and strong by hurting the other person and making the other person feel frightened or bad about themselves.

Violence is a choice. Domestic violence is not caused by drink or drug use. Drinking and drugs can make the abuse worse, but they do not cause the abuse to happen.

Abusers might say that they are feeling stressed because of money issues or because they don't have a job. Lots of abusers will say they only behave like this because their girlfriend or boyfriend asks for it or deserves it because of something (s)he's done. But these are all excuses. No one deserves abuse.

Will I become an abuser?

Many children and young people who grow up with domestic violence in their homes are afraid that they will also become an abuser or a victim of domestic violence when they grow up.

This does not have to be true! There are many, many boys and girls who grow up in homes with domestic violence and do not turn into abusers or victims themselves.

It's really important to remember that you are in control of who you want to be and how you want to behave.

Talk to someone you trust about what you've seen, what your worries are and what's happening. It's normal to feel angry and confused sometimes, but it's how you express your feelings that matters. You can learn about ways of behaving that are not abusive.

■ The Hideout is the first national website to support children and young people living with domestic violence.

Reproduced with permission from Women's Aid.

© The Women's Aid Federation of England 2005 (www.thehideout.org.uk)

Troubles at home kept secret by children

Information from the NSPCC

Children living with domestic violence, or whose parents have severe health problems, including drug and alcohol misuse, often say they want someone they can talk to whom they trust. But a report for the Joseph Rowntree Foundation warns that they rarely seek professional help to begin with – and that their experiences when they do have contact with support services are mixed.

It also suggests that children worry about their parents more than may be realised – especially if they fear for their parents' safety – and that boys find it especially hard to talk about their problems. The sadness and isolation that children experience can be perpetuated by the stigma and secrecy surrounding domestic violence, parental substance misuse and poor mental or physical health.

The review by Sarah Gorin, Senior Research Officer at the NSPCC, draws out key messages from 40 different research studies where children and young adults were interviewed, and another 50 related books and journal articles. It finds that:

- Children are often more aware of problems than their parents realise, but don't always understand what is happening, or why. Children's most persistent plea is for information that will help them understand what is going on in their family.
- Children whose parents have experienced domestic violence, substance misuse and, to a lesser extent, mental health problems, report witnessing or experiencing violence themselves. Their fear of violence is made worse by the unpredictability of their parents' moods and feeling like they are 'walking on eggshells'.

- Some children report feeling depressed, having difficulty making friends and experiencing problems at school, including bullying. Even so, the research concerned with domestic violence suggests that they can prove to be remarkably resilient and capable of healing their emotional wounds from bad experiences over time.
- In spite of their experiences, children frequently describe close relationships with parents and a strong sense of love and loyalty. Some are clearly torn between love for their parents and a dislike of their behaviour, or the restrictions placed on their own lives by their parents' problems.

Children are often more aware of problems than their parents realise, but don't always understand what is happening

---

Looking at children's coping strategies and sources of help and support, the review finds that many children try to 'blank out' their problems at home when they are with other people and find other ways of distracting themselves. This makes it even harder for teachers or health and social workers to identify them and offer support.

When children do talk about their experiences they are most likely to seek informal support through family and friends – or even talk to their pets – rather than first approach a professional. Accounts of receiving professional help vary, but many children in the research described negative experiences. They complained that professionals did not always talk to them in ways they could understand and, in some domestic violence cases, did not speak directly to them at all.

Sarah Gorin said: 'Lack of communication is a major barrier to children getting the help they need. Within families it often results from a shared desire to protect one another as well as a sense of secrecy and shame. Children also want to be believed and respected by professionals and involved in decision-making. Not talking to them may only make their sense of confusion, isolation and frustration worse.'

Mary Marsh, Director of the NSPCC, said: 'Talking about problems at home can be hard for some children and young people. We need to make sure that young people can confide in someone they trust, without fear of being told what to do or being judged or doubted.

'If young people really feel there is no one to turn to, they shouldn't despair. Advice and support is available from organisations such as the NSPCC who can help them come to terms with their problems and work out what to do next.'

- Information from the NSPCC – visit www.nspcc.org.uk for more.

Silence is not always golden

Tackling domestic violence in schools

What is domestic violence?

Domestic violence is an ongoing pattern of abusive or controlling behaviour and is widespread. It is rarely a one-off event; it tends over time to increase in frequency and severity. Domestic violence occurs irrespective of background and circumstance, race or ethnicity, sexuality, age, or disability and the overwhelming majority of victims are female and abusers male.

The Government definition of domestic violence is, 'any incident of threatening behaviour, violence or abuse – psychological, physical, sexual, financial or emotional – between adults who are or have been intimate partners or family members, regardless of gender or sexuality'.

This definition replaces the various definitions used by Government departments and agencies. The definition is supported by an explanatory text that makes it clear that domestic violence includes female genital mutilation, forced marriage and so-called 'honour crimes'.

The Crown Prosecution Service recognises that 'domestic violence' is a general term to describe a range of behaviour often used by one person to control and dominate another with whom they have, or have had, a close or family relationship. The CPS Policy on Domestic Violence applies when dealing with criminal offences that occur in a domestic context involving victims and abusers whatever their age, because of the importance of victim's and children's safety and defendant accountability.

Different forms of violence against women

These guidelines focus on domestic violence. Violence against women in the United Kingdom, however,

includes rape and sexual assault from strangers, sexual harassment, so-called 'honour' crimes, female genital mutilation, trafficking, forced prostitution and forced marriage. Victims may experience several forms of abuse at the same time; for example, forced marriage is a form of domestic violence that may involve sexual assault or rape and the threat of 'honour killing'.

Reunite International estimates that 1000 British Asian girls are forced into marriage against their will each year. Police in London receive 2 calls per week from women and girls reporting so-called 'honour crimes', such as being forced into marriage or being threatened with murder by their families.

Forced marriages, i.e. marriages conducted without the full consent of both parties and under duress, are not part of any religion and should not be confused with arranged marriages. It should be remembered that this issue is not solely an issue, as is commonly perceived, for British Asian communities. In England and Wales, there are cases involving families with origins in East Asia, the Middle East, Europe and Africa. The DfES and the Home Office has published guidance for education professionals setting out the 'warning signs' of students forced into marriage against their will.

A video has been produced jointly by the Foreign and Commonwealth Office and the DfES which gives school staff information on how to deal with forced marriage cases.

Why focus preventative work in schools?

Research on children and domestic violence has demonstrated not only that it is perfectly possible to talk to

children and young people about interpersonal violence but also that there is a great need to do so.

This is because young people are confused about the issue and want to learn more, and because those children who have lived with violence want to talk about it and make sense of their experiences. For all young people, whether or not they have lived with violence, peers emerge as an important source of support. Young people often find it easier to talk to their friends than to adults and discussing the issues together may be their favoured way of learning.

Research shows that prevention work in schools should start at or prior to the age 11, before attitudes begin to harden. Schools are perfect places to work with children and young people while they form their ideas about relationships. The aim should be to prevent violence from being a feature in their lives, rather than to intervene after the event.

The belief that children and young people who live with violence are themselves most likely to grow up to be violent is not substantiated by research. Indeed, children who have seen the impact of abuse are often strongly opposed to the repetition of such patterns in their own adult lives.

Tackling domestic violence through the curriculum

Attitudes towards women and girls that regard them as inferior to men and boys lie at the heart of most domestic violence. Within a broader context of schools' work on respect and conflict resolution, work needs to focus on gender stereotypes, on mutual respect in intimate relationships, and on challenging the condoning of domestic violence. Work on school culture and the prevention of bullying can usefully incorporate work on homophobic and racist abuse, as well as sexist bullying. It should always retain a focus on the causes of domestic violence as an essential element.

Research recognises that violence perpetrated against women is one of the ways in which male power is used to control women. It is these underlying attitudes that can be challenged by schools as part of the

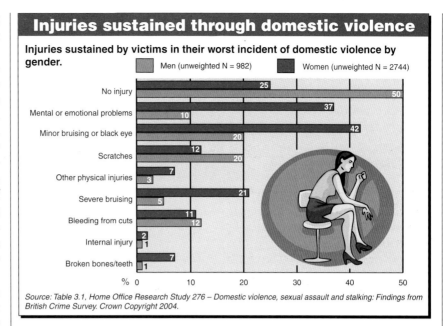

Injuries sustained through domestic violence

Injuries sustained by victims in their worst incident of domestic violence by gender.

Men (unweighted N = 982) Women (unweighted N = 2744)

Injury	Men (%)	Women (%)
No injury	25	50
Mental or emotional problems	10	37
Minor bruising or black eye	20	42
Scratches	12	20
Other physical injuries	7	3
Severe bruising	5	21
Bleeding from cuts	11	12
Internal injury	2	1
Broken bones/teeth	7	1

Source: Table 3.1, Home Office Research Study 276 – Domestic violence, sexual assault and stalking: Findings from British Crime Survey. Crown Copyright 2004.

whole school ethos. A study of educational programmes by the University of Warwick for Womankind Worldwide has shown that the issue should be addressed on a continuing basis otherwise the effect evaporates within a year. Tackling sexism and violence against women should therefore be part of the whole school culture and not a 'one-off' exercise.

Attitudes towards women and girls that regard them as inferior to men and boys lie at the heart of most domestic violence

---

Learning can spread far beyond Personal Social and Health Education into specific subject areas such as Drama and English and potentially to every area of the curriculum. It is highly relevant to Citizenship education, for example in relation to valuing people equally, respecting the law, and being a good citizen. There are also obvious links with equal opportunities policies in individual schools.

Teachers and governors need preparation and training before such work is undertaken. Targeted work by schools could lead to an increase in disclosures. Schools should establish close working links with agencies in the domestic violence

field; some local Women's Aid Organisations work with schools to provide domestic violence training and support for children in schools and many local authorities have domestic violence support officers for schools.

The Children Act 2004 established a duty on local authorities to make arrangements to promote co-operation between agencies in order to improve children's well-being. 'Well-being' is defined by the Government in its Every Child Matters policies by reference to five outcomes: being healthy; staying safe; enjoying and achieving; making a positive contribution; and achieving economic well-being. This new duty will commence on 1 April 2005. More details on these changes are at: www.everychildmatters.gov.uk.

Citizenship, Sex and Relationships Education and Personal Social and Health Education and specific subject areas provide opportunities for teachers to raise awareness of domestic violence and to encourage discussion and debate. Through the wider curriculum and particularly through Citizenship and Personal Social and Health Education, schools can seek to:

- consider concepts of power within relationships and how these can lead to violence in the home;
- address the gender stereotypes that continue to exist surrounding 'male' and 'female' behaviour, characteristics, and skills;

One in three child protection cases shows a history of domestic violence to the mother

- challenge the attitudes that can lead to violent behaviour;
- inform pupils about the reasons why women can be forced to stay with violent partners such as financial insecurity, threats against their children or family or depression and mental health problems;
- discuss ways of making relationships work effectively such as the need for communication and listening;
- inform pupils about the legal consequences of domestic violence and that it is against the law;
- provide information on the fact that there are a range of organisations and agencies who can assist the victims of domestic violence; and
- organise events to celebrate the White Ribbon Campaign, which runs through November, leading up to the 25th, which is White Ribbon Day (International Day Against Violence Against Women).

What can schools do to challenge gender stereotypes?

It is important that schools consistently play an active role in challenging prejudice, gender stereotyping and discrimination against women.

Sexist language and playground banter that seeks to legitimise violence against women should be challenged. Schools should consider the following challenges:

- how they can enlist the help of parents/carers in questioning stereotypes;
- the role of pupils and students in taking forward gender issues;
- to what extent gender issues are included in policy planning and development;
- how behaviour policies impact on girls and boys;
- whether they are doing everything possible to make classrooms and teaching spaces welcoming to both sexes and to use resources that are free from gender bias;
- how the ethos takes account of female and male pupils, students and teachers;
- how they may challenge traditional attitudes to career routes and work placements for boys and girls; and
- their response to instances of sexist bullying and name calling and whether gender violence is covered in policies on bullying.

Violence against women often means violence against families

Statistics confirm the strong link between domestic violence and child abuse. One in three child protection cases shows a history of domestic violence to the mother. Children living with domestic violence are three to nine times more likely to be injured and abused, either directly or while trying to protect a parent.

In a significant number of cases women and their children are abused by the same adult male perpetrator in the family. There are, however, other patterns of child abuse, some of which include women as abusers.

In some cases of domestic violence the perpetrator may use children as a way of controlling and manipulating the mother and to stop her from seeking help and support. Women often do not report domestic violence because they fear that they may lose their children.

Impact on children

Children can be affected in many ways by living with domestic violence. There is no set pattern of signs or symptoms. It is widely accepted that there are dramatic and serious effects of children witnessing domestic violence, which can result in behavioural problems, absenteeism, ill health, bullying, anti-social behaviour, drug and alcohol misuse, self-harm and psychosocial impacts. The extent to which even very young children can be aware of violence and of the long-term damaging effects on a child's health, educational attainment and emotional well-being, is frequently underestimated.

Children living with domestic violence are three to nine times more likely to be injured and abused, either directly or while trying to protect a parent

Moving from former family homes to new accommodation may mean changes of school. Change of school can be a difficult time for a family but the particular circumstances associated with escape from domestic violence can make it even more difficult, particularly if there is a delay before a school place can be found. If a mother changes her address often or enters a refuge to escape her violent partner, social isolation and loss of friends add to the insecurity of children.

- The above information is an extract from *Silence is not always golden – tackling domestic violence* (London, NUT), providing guidelines for teaching on domestic violence in schools. To view the whole text, visit the National Union of Teachers' website which can be found at www.teachers.org.uk

© NUT

Domestic violence – in their words

Billy

'I don't always know where mum is – if she runs to a refuge and it takes time to get in touch.'

Billy's mum was often beaten by her partner and frequently spent time in a refuge. She always returned home. Billy experienced a great deal of violence at home and as a result he is very timid and easily frightened.

The experience of domestic violence left Billy vulnerable and he could be taken advantage of extremely easily. Eventually, he was taken into care, but still suffered a great deal of stress worrying about his mother and what was going on at home. This situation intensified when Billy's mum was forced to flee the violence, as it often took time before she could get in touch with him.

Now 17, Billy has learning difficulties and is living in supported lodgings, helped by Barnardo's Signpost Project. 'The scars from domestic violence are frequently there for long periods of time', says the service leader at Signpost. 'The children and young people who have experienced it often show signs of what has happened to them – they look nervous and unsettled; some even flinch if you lean toward them.'

'Domestic violence can affect children in different ways. Some become withdrawn and tearful. Some have poor self-esteem and lack trust or confidence. Others become aggressive or bullying because they think this is normal behaviour.'

Billy is very responsive to the help he gets, but his previous experience is difficult to overcome. He finds it hard to manage the simple daily tasks of shopping, cooking and managing money. He also finds it hard to confide in people.

'These children and young people can live in a fantasy world – for some it's their way of managing it all. They put themselves in a bubble and everything outside that bubble they won't look at or listen to. Often they blame themselves.'

Andrew

'Dad hit mum, so she drank. She tried to lock him out the house, but he said he'd burn it down while we were asleep.'

Andrew's family had lived in fear of his father for as long as he could remember, and seeing his mother beaten was a regular event. Terrified and depressed, she drank to dull the pain. If she tried to lock Andrew's father out of the house, he would threaten to commit suicide, or burn the house down in the night – with all the family inside. He threatened to tell the local authority that she couldn't cope with her children.

Andrew's frustrations boiled over in school and at home. He made a constant nuisance of himself on the estate where he lived and there were regular complaints to the police. At school he was difficult to control, swearing at teachers and intimidating his classmates. Violence was a way of life. He was regularly excluded from school, and the family faced eviction.

Andrew was then referred to Barnardo's Matrix Project, which identified Andrew's fear of his father and an environment of violence as key factors in his behaviour. He was encouraged to develop new skills to deal with confrontation instead of fighting or storming out of school.

The Service also supported Andrew's mother, helping her with parenting skills. As her confidence developed, she found the courage to leave with her children. With the threat of violence removed, she was able to control her drinking.

'I just didn't think that I could be a good mother after all we had been through', she said. 'He took away the belief I had in myself. But I've found the confidence to take responsibility for all of our lives. It's down to me now.'

■ Information from Barnardo's – visit www.barnardos.org.uk for more, or see page 41 for address details.

© Barnardo's

Domestic violence – its effects on children

Information from the Royal College of Psychiatrists

What is domestic violence?

The term 'domestic violence' is used to describe the physical, sexual or emotional (including verbal and financial) abuse inflicted on a man or woman by their partner or ex-partner.

How are children involved?

In relationships where there is domestic violence, children witness about three-quarters of the abusive incidents. About half the children in such families have themselves been badly hit or beaten. Sexual and emotional abuse are also more likely to happen in these families.

How are children affected?

Obviously it is very upsetting for children to see one of their parents (or partners) abusing or attacking the other. They often show signs of great distress.

Younger children may become anxious, complain of tummy-aches or start to wet their bed. They may find it difficult to sleep, have temper tantrums and start to behave as if they are much younger than they are.

Older children react differently. Boys seem to express their distress much more outwardly. They may become aggressive and disobedient. Sometimes, they start to use violence to try and solve problems, as if they have learnt to do this from the way that adults behave in their family. Older boys may play truant and may start to use alcohol or drugs.

Girls are more likely to keep their distress inside. They may withdraw from other people and become anxious or depressed. They may think badly of themselves and complain of vague physical symptoms. They are more likely to have an eating disorder, or to harm themselves by taking overdoses or cutting themselves.

Children with these problems often do badly at school. They may also get symptoms of post-traumatic stress disorder, for example have nightmares and flashbacks, and be easily startled.

Are there any long-term effects?

Yes. Children who have witnessed violence are more likely to be either abusers or victims themselves. Children tend to copy the behaviour of their parents. Boys learn from their fathers to be violent to women. Girls learn from their mothers that violence is to be expected, and something you just have to put up with.

Children don't always repeat the same pattern when they grow up. Many children don't like what they see, and try very hard not to make the same mistakes as their parents. Even so, children from violent families often grow up feeling anxious and depressed, and find it difficult to get on with other people.

What can help?

- Professionals working with children, including doctors, nurses, teachers and social workers, should make themselves available for the child to talk to, and offer the help and advice they need.
- Posters in community centres, schools and health centres can give information and guidance.
- Women's Aid and Victim Support are national organisations that give information and support.
- Legal advice is often important – the law has recently been changed to make it easier to get.

People in general need to recognise how harmful domestic violence is to children. This can help the victims of violence to realise that it shouldn't be happening to them, and that they can ask for help.

Who can give mothers and children long-term help?

Help is often needed for a long time. Survival needs have top priority – safety from the abuse, a place to live, and money to live on. Then for the children involved, contact arrangements and school need to be sorted out. The mother is likely to be extremely stressed and may well need her own counselling, psychotherapy or treatment for depression or anxiety. Children showing difficulties in school often need extra help from teachers. If the children continue to be emotionally disturbed, it may be helpful for them to be seen at the local child and adolescent mental health service or some other local family and child counselling service.

■ The above information is reprinted with kind permission from the Royal College of Psychiatrists and is part of a range of factsheets entitled 'Mental Health and Growing Up'. See www.rcpsych.ac.uk/info/mhgu for more information, or see page 41 for address details.

© Royal College of Psychiatrists

Alarm at acceptance of abuse by teenage girls

**By John Carvel
and Steven Morris**

Many teenage girls are caught up in a cycle of violence, experiencing abuse at home before becoming victims of attacks from aggressive boyfriends, a survey reveals today (21 March 2005).

One in three girls and young women who had been hit by their parents went on to be abused by their boyfriends, according to the survey, which is backed by the children's charity the NSPCC.

An acceptance of violence also emerged in the survey of 2,000 teenagers aged 13-19, with more than four in 10 (43%) believing it was acceptable for a boyfriend to get aggressive in certain circumstances – for example if a girl cheated on him, flirted with somebody else, screamed at him or 'dressed outrageously'.

One in six teenage girls surveyed said they had been hit by their boyfriends, 4% of them regularly

Child protection experts expressed alarm that the survey, undertaken by the teen magazine *Sugar*, seemed to show that many teenage girls appeared to think violence was an acceptable, even normal, part of everyday life.

Wes Cuell, director of services to children and young people at the charity, described the statistics as 'scary'.

He said: 'There is a view that young people today are more sassy, able to take care of themselves. This survey shows that is not the case. Young people are increasingly vulnerable. The survey reveals a generation of girls, many of whom are growing up believing that aggression is an acceptable part of life.'

Annabel Brog, the magazine's editor, said: 'An appalling number of girls feel violence at home or in relationships is sometimes acceptable. They need to know that nobody has the right to hurt them, scare them or abuse them in any way.'

Julie Bindel, founder of Justice for Women, said that in her experience abused young women did not accept violence, but did not have the power to stop it, often because they had come into contact with violence from early age.

She said: 'It's not that they think violence is normal. It's that they don't have the resources to deal with it. Predatory men target women who are vulnerable.'

A third of the girls and young women who took part in the survey said they had experienced violence at home.

One-fifth said they had been hit by parents, a quarter of them regularly.

But more than half of the girls who saw parents hitting each other or screaming and shouting did not regard this as 'domestic violence'.

However, the impact on the girls was plain from the survey. Only 9% of girls regularly hit by parents described themselves as having 'lots of self-confidence'. Girls hit regularly were more likely to describe themselves as 'insecure and quiet'.

One in six of those surveyed said they had been hit by their boyfriends, 4% of them regularly. Another 15% had been pushed. Two-thirds of them said they had stayed with the boyfriend after being hit or pushed.

More than 40% of girls said they would consider giving a boy a second chance if he hit them. Six per cent simply said it was acceptable for a boy to hit his girlfriend and 2% could 'understand' a boy forcing his girlfriend to have sex in certain circumstances.

The link between violence at home and within relationships is stark.

Around a third of girls hit regularly by their boyfriends said they had seen their parents hit one another. A third of the young women who had been hit by their parents went on to be hit by boyfriends.

Also highlighted in the survey were regional variations. More teenage girls in the Midlands and Scotland said boyfriends had hit them (19%), while more Welsh girls had been forced into sex (10%).

Fewer of the girls from London and the south-east said a boyfriend who hit his girlfriend should be given a second chance (36%).

The NSPCC may commission more research into the regional variations so that it could tailor messages to specific areas.

The figures revealed in the survey are broadly in line with the statistics for adult victims.

According to the Home Office, one in four women and one in six men suffer from domestic violence at some point in their lives.

Every year around 150 people are killed by a current or former partner and domestic abuse accounts for 16% of all violent crime. It also has more repeat offenders' victims than any other crime – on average there will be 35 assaults before a victim calls the police.

Campaigners claim a more strategic approach to eradicating domestic violence is needed.

Last month the Crown Prosecution Service published new guidelines on how to deal with cases, which included advice on when an allegation should be tested in court, even if the victim has said she or he wants it dropped.

And they all lived happily ever after . . . ?

Information from the University of Derby

Girls who hear fairytale classics such as *Cinderella* and *Beauty and the Beast* when they are children are more likely to stay in destructive relationships as adults, new research has revealed.

'Love won't always find a way,' says psychotherapist Susan Darker-Smith. Victims of domestic violence repeatedly tell her that they believe 'if their love is strong enough they can change their partner's behaviour' and many identify with the characters in the stories.

Susan's research shows that girls who grow up in homes where they are read bedtime stories identify with the book characters as role models. These characters provide them with a template for future submissive behaviour.

Susan, who is studying for her Masters in Cognitive Behavioural Psychotherapy at the University of Derby, interviewed domestic violence victims and parents of primary school children in Leicester for her research.

UNIVERSITY *of* DERBY

Parents' most popular bedtime story choices for girls are *Cinderella* and *Rapunzel*, while the boys are more likely to listen to *Paddington Bear* and *Thomas the Tank Engine*.

Susan said: 'Girls who have listened to such stories as children tend to become more submissive in their future relationships.'

She feels the advent of television is exposing children to different stimuli. Coupled with having less literature read to them, Susan says children could grow up to be less submissive than the current generation.

Three abstracts of Susan's work are to be read at the International Congress of Cognitive Therapy in Gothenburg, Sweden, next month (June 2005).

The study, 'The Tales We Tell Our Children – or over conditioning of girls to expect partners to change', will be read out to the world's most influential therapists including Cognitive Behavioural Therapy founder Aaron Beck.

Margaret Smith, who runs the Prevention of Domestic Abuse Centre at the University of Derby, said: 'We learn about ourselves and how we relate to others through stories in childhood.

'If we hold these beliefs deeply enough, and have submissive personalities as adults, it can be difficult to break away from destructive relationships.'

Susan's other two abstracts are set to spark further interest in the fields of anorexia and post-traumatic stress respectively.

'The Dual Mind-Set Of Anorexia Nervosa – conceptualism through to cure' looks at how anorexic victims often enjoy creative pursuits and struggle with mathematics – yet are able to become experts in weight and calorie calculation very rapidly.

Susan suggests an imbalance between the left side of the brain (critical) and the right side (creative) intensifies anorexia and could be treated by compassionate mind training currently being used to help schizophrenics.

Victims of domestic violence repeatedly tell [Susan Darker-Smith] that they believe 'if their love is strong enough they can change their partner's behaviour' and many identify with the characters in the stories

---

'The Disappearing Self – or post-traumatic stress disorder and identity in domestic violence survivors' suggests a new model for emotional trauma which looks at emotional age resetting in trauma survivors, relative to how long ago the abuse occurred.

Susan, who hopes to move on to study a clinical doctorate at the University of Derby, received EARP funding, a grant from the University of Derby, and financial assistance from the Leicester-based Sir Thomas White charity.

■ Information courtesy of the University of Derby. Please visit the website www.derby.ac.uk for more information, or see page 41 for their address details.

© University of Derby 2005

Freephone 24-hour National Domestic Violence Helpline

Run in partnership between Women's Aid and Refuge

You can contact the Freephone 24-Hour National Domestic Violence Helpline on 0808 2000 247

The Helpline is a member of Language Line and can provide access to an interpreter for non-English-speaking callers. The Helpline can also access the BT Type Talk Service for deaf callers

The Helpline provides support, information and a listening ear to women experiencing (or who have experienced) domestic abuse and to those seeking help on a woman's behalf. Helpline staff will discuss the available options and, if appropriate, refer callers on to refuges and other sources of help and information. Our aim is to enable women to discuss options for action and to empower them to make informed choices to change their life and their children's lives.

If you, or someone you know, is experiencing (or has experienced) physical, emotional, psychological or sexual abuse in the home, the Helpline can give you support, help

and information over the telephone for free, wherever you are in the country. All calls are taken in the strictest confidence.

In the year 2003/2004 the Freephone 24-Hour National Domestic Violence Helpline received in excess of 250,000 calls of which Women's Aid and Refuge dealt with approximately 74,000. In 2005 the Helpline continues to receive very high call volumes from women who are or who have been experiencing domestic violence, their family members, friends, work colleagues and professionals working on their behalf. When all the lines are busy there is a voicemail service that enables callers to leave a message. The voicemail is checked regularly throughout each day and calls are returned as soon as possible.

The Helpline is staffed 24hrs a day by fully trained Helpline support workers and volunteers. All staff are

women. During the course of a call, the Helpline support worker will respond according to the caller's needs. They may for example:

- Offer a supportive listening ear and (if appropriate) refer to counselling services.
- Refer women experiencing domestic abuse to a registered family law solicitor in her area.
- Refer women to local, face-to-face support via the drop-in or outreach services provided by their local domestic violence service.
- Refer women (with or without children) to emergency accommodation.
- Send callers a Women's Aid information pack, with leaflets from a selection that cover a range of issues such as Housing, Legal, Myths, Risks to children, Health and Domestic violence, Breaking Free.

The Helpline also responds individually to letters and emails from women experiencing domestic abuse or friends/relatives/professionals seeking information on her behalf.

- Women's Aid is the national domestic violence charity which co-ordinates and supports an England-wide network of over 300 local projects, providing over 500 refuges, helplines, outreach services and advice centres. Our work is built on almost 30 years of campaigning and developing new responses to domestic violence.

Reproduced with kind permission from Women's Aid – for more visit www.womensaid.org.uk

© *The Women's Aid Federation of England 2004 (www.womensaid.org.uk)*

The safe house

Where do you go when you leave an abusive relationship? Helen Gent reports on the work of women's refuges and explains how to find a safe house near you

Right now, as you read this article, 7,000 women and children are staying in refuges in England. Broaden the picture to the whole of the UK, and the annual figure for refuge-seekers is 63,000. If you find those statistics disturbing, look away now, because you won't want to hear the stories behind them. The tales of women who are punched, kicked, slapped and beaten by abusive husbands and partners. Women who are bruised, broken and defeated. Women who die. Because for every woman who has finally found the strength to leave, there's another still trapped in a living hell at home.

Domestic violence: the facts

'You can't use the number of women staying in refuges, or even contacting a refuge, as a picture of the extent of domestic violence,' says Nicola Harwin, of the national domestic violence charity Women's Aid. In the absence of any national study all you can do, she says, is look to the smaller research samples which, time and again, have produced the same alarming facts. That one in four women, for instance, will experience domestic violence during their lifetime. Or that one in nine will be experiencing it NOW. 'That's one in nine women too many,' asserts Nicola. 'It proves that domestic violence is still a huge social problem which isn't being adequately addressed.'

Money matters

You have only to look at the number of refuges available to women in the UK – currently 400 – to realise that help for victims of domestic abuse is few and far between. Not surprisingly, funding – or rather the lack of it – is a major issue. Most refuge organisations, who provide not just safe houses but other services such as drop-in centres and outreach services, exist as charities and are therefore reliant on fund-raising to keep them operating.

Even Women's Aid, which is recognised as the national co-ordinating body for refuge services, gets minimal government funding to run its national domestic violence helpline – a service that has dealt with 32,000 calls in the past six months alone.

Changing the rules

But lack of funding isn't the only issue here. While it's true that the police and other organisations are more attuned to the problem of domestic violence, often a lack of co-ordination means women's safety can be put in jeopardy even after they've got into a refuge.

> *You have only to look at the number of refuges available to women in the UK – currently 400 – to realise that help for victims of domestic abuse is few and far between*

As Nicola Harwin explains: 'Many women's safety is compromised by family courts that deal with arrangements for contact with fathers. It's all very well the Home Office encouraging crime reduction strategies to take on board domestic violence, but it's no good if two weeks after a woman has gone to a refuge she's being forced to meet her abuser once a week to hand over her child for a contact visit.' This glaring contradiction in government policy is something Women's Aid is currently trying to address.

Fighting back

While refuge organisations continue to fight for funding and greater awareness, the good news is that websites like Women's Aid and iVillage are helping women to win their own battles against domestic violence. They are showing women like 80-year-old Ethel – a victim for most of her married life – that there is a way out of the bullying. 'I've got a computer in my bedroom, you see,' says Ethel. 'I know how to work it but my husband doesn't. So now I can find out my rights.' One woman, beaten but not defeated. It's still not enough.

How to seek help

Finding a refuge
The Women's Aid 24-hour National Domestic Violence Helpline (08457 023 468) has a list of refuges, and they will either pass on the telephone numbers or, if you'd prefer, will contact a refuge on your behalf. You can also contact refuges through the Samaritans, the police, social services or the Citizens Advice Bureau.

Some women prefer to stay in a local refuge, while others may wish to move away from an area. If space isn't available at your preferred refuge, you will be offered another refuge or alternative local authority emergency accommodation. Refuges take children. Contact details for refuges in your local area are available on the Women's Aid website.

What to take
'If you are thinking about leaving, you need to do some action and safety planning because there are lots of practical things you'll need,' says Nicola Harwin. The checklist includes paperwork such as ID, birth certificate, passport and driving licence, personal effects such as family photos plus toiletries for yourself and your children. What you

You need to discuss this, along with any concerns about joint property and mortgage arrangements, with a member of staff as soon as possible. They will be able to advise you on the best course of action.

Further information

To find a refuge, call the Women's Aid 24-hour National Domestic Helpline on 08457 023 468 or go to www.womensaid.org. You do not have to be in an emergency situation to contact the helpline for advice and support. Local Women's Aid services also offer drop-in and outreach services.

■ The above information is reproduced with the permission of iVillage Ltd – for more information visit the website at www.ivillage.co.uk

© iVillage Ltd 2005

don't need, stresses Nicola, is any evidence to show that you have been abused. However it might be useful to have details of any other agencies you have told about your experiences (GP, social worker, etc), as this could help with proceedings in the Family Court.

At the refuge

Rest assured that refuge addresses are confidential and once you're there you can stay as long as you need to. Refuges vary in size and some are for particular ethnic or cultural backgrounds – many have disabled access. At most refuges you will be given your own bedroom along with communal use of a living room and kitchen plus a shared bathroom. Some refuges do provide self-contained family units.

How to pay

Refuges couldn't run without a rental income – women are asked to pay between £90 and £350 a week for space, depending on circumstances. However, you won't have to pay any money upfront. Instead, when you arrive at the refuge, you will be helped to make a claim for income support and housing benefit. 'Women will absolutely not be expected to hand over money when they arrive,' says Nicola. 'A lot of women come to refuges with no money on them, and the first task is to get them emergency payment from social security.' However, if you are in regular employment but have left your job in order to move into a refuge, your rights to benefit could be affected.

Male victims of domestic violence

Information from SupportLine

If you are a male victim of domestic violence, you may have found it difficult to find adequate help and support. Unfortunately there is still a belief among some that men simply cannot be victims of domestic violence. This can make it even more difficult for male victims to confide in anyone about what is happening which can lead to depression, despair, low self-esteem, a feeling of hopelessness and isolation.

If you are a man who is being abused in this way there ARE people out there who can offer support, understanding, information, advice, help! People who will not ignore or dismiss what is happening to you, but people who will genuinely care and want to be there for you in whatever way they can.

If you are a victim of domestic violence there are some steps you can take:

- Keep a diary of all incidents of abuse with dates, times and details of the abuse.
- If you receive any injuries report this to your doctor and ensure that you tell him this was due to domestic violence.
- If possible get photos of the injuries.
- Don't leave home unless you are threatened (unless the situation is so bad that you need to leave for the sake of your health, safety, and state of mind).
- Do try and tell family and friends exactly what is happening and do not cover up the abuse and/or make excuses for your partner.
- If you are provoked do try not to retaliate otherwise your partner can manipulate this to look as though she/he is the injured party.
- Seek legal advice as soon as possible.
- Seek emotional support/counselling as soon as possible.

■ The above information is provided courtesy of SupportLine – for details of agencies who can offer support and information to male victims of domestic violence, please visit the domestic violence page on their website at www.supportline.org.uk/problems/domesticViolence.php or call their helpline on (020) 8554 9004.

© SupportLine

Contacting Women's Aid

Information from Welsh Women's Aid

Important things to remember when contacting Women's Aid

If you contact Women's Aid by telephone remember to dial 141 before the area code. This will stop anyone who uses the telephone straight after you from finding out who you have called by pressing redial.

However, if you have an itemised telephone bill the Women's Aid number may be listed. It is therefore a good idea to telephone Women's Aid from a telephone other than your home such as a telephone box, a friend's telephone or your mobile telephone (if it is safe from your abuser).

Most Women's Aid groups may not ring you at home in case it is not safe to do so. So if possible arrange for them to call you back at a friend's house, on a mobile telephone or on a public payphone that accepts incoming calls.

What happens when you contact the On Call service?

All member groups operate a 24-hour On Call service. This means that they can be contacted at any time day or night.

You can contact any of the Women's Aid groups in Wales individually. All their numbers are available on this website, in yellow pages or by telephoning directory enquiries on 118 118.

(Women's Aid in Wales does not have a national helpline number but one is being planned with support from the Welsh Assembly Government.)

The worker who answers your call will always be a woman and is a trained Women's Aid worker.

She will explain that you are not alone and that lots of women and children are in a similar situation to yours. She will listen and give you time to talk. She will not expect or insist that you give her more information than you want to.

The On Call worker will explain what Women's Aid does and how they can help you.

She can arrange for you to go into a refuge if that is what you want to do.

You may not feel ready to come into refuge just yet or you may not want to come into refuge at all. That is perfectly OK.

The On Call worker is there for you to talk to for as long as you need. If her group has an information centre she will give the address, phone number and times when you can drop in and talk face to face with a Women's Aid worker if you want to.

You can contact the On Call service as often as you like and will be able to talk to someone who understands your situation and will not judge or blame you.

What happens when you decide to live in a refuge?

Any woman who is escaping domestic abuse can go into refuge regardless of her marital status, sexuality and whether or not she has children. A refuge offers safe temporary accomodation until you are able to find alternative permanent housing for yourself and your family (if any).

You can ask to go into a refuge either by phoning the Women's Aid On Call number, visiting the Women's Aid Information Centre or Outreach service or you can get another agency such as the police or other agency to refer you.

When a Women's Aid group is contacted to say you want to go into refuge that group will find space for you in one of the refuges across Wales.

Some women will want to move a long way away from their home while others will want to remain as near as possible.

You can arrange to move into refuge immediately but space cannot be booked as we offer emergency accommodation only. We cannot guarantee that space will be available in any particular refuge at any time and groups often will not place a woman from their town in their own refuge for obvious safety reasons.

If you decide to come in to refuge, the Women's Aid workers will need some information:

- your name (you can just give your first name)
- a telephone number where you can be contacted safely e.g. your mobile phone, or a friend's telephone
- if you have any children and if so their ages and gender
- the area in which you live
- if you have your own transport. If not she will arrange for you to be collected by taxi or a Women's Aid worker
- where you can be collected from.

She will also suggest items that you should bring with you if possible.

When you first go into refuge a worker will show you your room and the rest of the refuge. (In some groups you might be greeted by the other women in the house and shown round until a worker arrives, espe-

cially if it is at night.) You will be given a front-door key or swipe card so that you can go in and out.

You will be asked for quite a lot of information and will have to fill in forms but this is so that the group can start assisting you to sort things out (e.g. benefits) as soon as possible. Don't worry if you can't remember everything straight away or if you have problems with filling in forms, the workers are there to help you and understand that this is a very stressful and frightening time for you and your children.

The refuge will have emergency supplies such as food, spare clothes, nappies, baby milk and bottles. Bedding is always provided.

The worker will go through the refuge rules which are there to help to keep everyone safe. These rules also help all people living in the refuge to live together peacefully.

It is really important that you keep the address of the refuge secret. This is to protect everyone who lives and works there. It is best not to tell anyone where you are so that they can't pass on the information, even by mistake. There will be a phone in the refuge that you can use to let people know that you are safe.

The workers will assist you to sort out practical things such as health matters, education for your children, your employment, and so on, until you decide what your long-term plans are. You can stay in the refuge for as long as you need – days, weeks or months until you are ready to move out.

What to take with you into refuge

The following list is a guide to what you should try and take with you when you go into refuge but remember: if you are in any danger don't stop to collect belongings, just get you and your children out of the house.

The Women's Aid workers can always arrange for you to return to your home with a police escort or for someone else to collect your belongings.

- ID such as driving licence, marriage certificate, passport
- prescribed medication
- birth certificates for you and your children

- benefit books
- money, credit cards, cheque book and card, building society pass-books
- house/car/work keys
- medical cards
- address book
- mobile phone
- mortgage/rent documents
- your children's favourite items such as teddy, blanket, dummy, clothing
- clothes, shoes, coats and toiletries for you and your children.

You will not be able to take furniture with you as the refuge is furnished but the group may be able to help you to arrange storage for some items. Pets are usually not allowed in refuges but groups may know of or have arrangements with local pet fostering schemes.

What happens when you visit an information centre?

A Women's Aid group's information centre is separate from the refuge.

It will have set opening hours in the same way as a Citizens' Advice Bureau.

You can drop in without an appointment but it might be a good idea to phone first if possible.

In the same way as when a woman contacts the On Call service the workers at the information centre, who are always women, are there to listen. They see women and children every day who are experiencing domestic abuse and they will explain that you are not alone and that there are many women and children in similar situations.

The worker will explain what Women's Aid does and how they can support you with whatever decisions you make.

They can offer to find you space in a refuge if that is what you want to do or arrange for you to talk to a worker again.

Women's Aid can give you information about:
- contacting a solicitor
- contacting the police and maybe contacting a local Domestic Violence officer
- if you have suffered physical abuse they can arrange for you to receive medical treatment
- contacting social services.

The Women's Aid workers will make sure that you have the group's 24-hour On Call number and explain how this works.

Women's Aid workers do not provide counselling. They are there to listen and help outline your immediate and long-term options and support you in whatever decision you make.

You can contact or visit the information centre as many times as you need to.

What happens when you contact the Outreach service?

Some Women's Aid groups have an Outreach service that supports women and children in their own home.

You can access support from a Women's Aid Outreach service by phoning the On Call number or dropping into the information centre and arranging to meet an Outreach worker.

If you have contacted the group either through the On Call service or by calling into the information centre, you can arrange to talk or meet with the outreach worker at a time and place that suits you both.

Some groups also have Outreach surgeries in venues such as medical or community centres. You can drop into one of these Outreach surgeries and meet and talk to a Women's Aid worker.

The Outreach worker can provide practical and emotional support to women either in their own homes, if this is safe, or in a neutral place such as a cafe.

The Outreach service can support you by:
- helping you to find somewhere safe to live
- sorting out new schools

- accompanying you to solicitors' appointments or court hearings
- putting you in touch with local support groups
- helping you to sort out financial problems
- listening and talking through your problems.

Improvements in the legal system now mean that some women and children may be able to stay in the family home with legal protection against the person who is abusing them.

Some women who are experiencing domestic abuse may not feel ready to leave the abusive situation, or indeed their home, but may want to talk about their situation with someone who understands but is not involved.

Other women may feel that they still need the support of Women's Aid when they have moved out of the refuge and back to the family home or have been rehoused.

Women moving into the community after their stay in refuge are generally new to the area and do not have the usual support of family and friends. Women may be worried about how they are going to cope and the Outreach worker can make all the difference to many women in this situation.

Many groups now have Outreach child workers who provide support for children and young people that have experienced domestic abuse and are living in the community.

- Information from Welsh Women's Aid – for more information visit www.welshwomensaid.org or see page 41 for contact details.

© *Welsh Women's Aid*

A friend in need

How can I help a friend who is experiencing domestic violence?

Unless you are attempting to assist someone who has been very open about their experiences it may be difficult for you to acknowledge the problem directly. However, there are some basic steps that you can take to assist a friend, family member, colleague, neighbour or anyone you know who confides in you that they are experiencing domestic abuse.

- Approach her in an understanding, non-blaming way. Explain to her that she is not alone and that there are many women like her in the same situation. Acknowledge that it takes strength to trust someone enough to talk to them about experiencing abuse. Give her time to talk; don't push her to go into too much detail if she doesn't want to.
- Acknowledge that she is in a scary, difficult situation. Tell her that no one deserves to be threatened or beaten, despite what her abuser has told her. Nothing she can do or say can justify the abuser's behaviour.
- Support her as a friend. Be a good listener. Encourage her to express her hurt and anger. Allow her to make her own decisions, even if it means she isn't ready to leave the relationship. This is her decision.

women's aid
until women & children are safe

- Ask if she has suffered physical harm. Offer to go with her to the hospital if she needs to go. Help her to report the assault to the police if she chooses to do so.
- Be ready to provide information on the help available to abused women and their children. Explore the available options with her. Go with her to visit a solicitor if she is ready to take this step.
- Plan safe strategies for leaving an abusive relationship. Let her create the boundaries of what is safe and what is not safe; don't encourage her to follow any strategies that she is expressing doubt about.
- Offer the use of your address and/or telephone number for information and messages relating to your friend's situation.
- Look after yourself while you are supporting someone through such a difficult and emotional time.

Ensure that you do not put yourself into a dangerous situation; for example, do not offer to talk to the abuser about your friend or let yourself be seen by the abuser as a threat to their relationship.

- Women's Aid is the national domestic violence charity which co-ordinates and supports an England-wide network of over 300 local projects, providing over 500 refuges, helplines, outreach services and advice centres. Our work is built on almost 30 years of campaigning and developing new responses to domestic violence.

Reproduced with kind permission from Women's Aid.

© *The Women's Aid Federation of England 2005 (www.womensaid.org.uk)*

How can I help my mum or dad?

'I really wanted to help my mum but I didn't know what to do. . .'

I want the abuse to stop

No matter who's hurting whom, it's important for you to remember that it's not your responsibility to protect your parent from the abuse. The abuse needs to stop, but no matter how strong you are it's not your responsibility to stop it. You can get help.

Some children and young people want their parents to stay together, but they want the violence to stop. This may or may not be possible. In any case, it's important that your parents get help, so that the abuse stops.

Why don't we leave?

You might wonder why your parent doesn't leave the abuse or why it carries on even though your parents have separated.

There are many reasons why someone might stay in an abusive relationship. It's possible that:

- They don't know where else to go.
- They may still love their partner.
- They hope their partner will change and the violence will stop.
- They don't want to take their children away from the other parent.
- They don't have the money to leave.

THE HIDEOUT
www.thehideout.org.uk
until children are safe

- They don't feel strong enough to leave. Because of the abuse they've stopped believing in themselves.

Just like you might feel mixed up about what's happening, your parent might also feel confused about what to do.

If you have questions about what's going on, don't be afraid to ask your parent who's being abused about it. Sometimes it's difficult for them to talk to you about the violence because they want to protect you. They might think you don't know about the fighting. If you want, try talking to your parent who's being abused about your worries, so they know how you're feeling.

Who can my mum or dad talk to?

There are helplines that your mum or dad can call to talk about their feelings and to get more information about what they can do. Visit The Hideout online for more information.

There are helplines for men and women – for abusers and for victims.

Where can we go?

If it's your mum who's being abused, she can try to move to a refuge, a safe house, with you and your brothers and sisters. Read more about this option in Moving to a refuge on our website.

Women and children don't have to move to a refuge to get help. Most areas now have local support services that know about domestic violence and that can help women, children and young people through this. They can offer advice, information and support about staying safe and about the options available to you and your family.

Some areas also have local support for men who want to change their behaviour and want to stop being violent. In our website's More help section we've included some helpline numbers for men to call to find out about support that is available to them.

- The Hideout is the first national website to support children and young people living with domestic violence.

Reproduced with kind permission from Women's Aid.

© The Women's Aid Federation of England 2005 (www.thehideout.org.uk)

Legal protection against domestic abuse

Protection for women and children experiencing domestic violence and abuse

For women and children fleeing domestic violence and abuse there is recourse to the criminal law and the protection of the police and courts.

There are a number of laws to protect women and children. These are:

- Children's Act 1989 (child protection)
- Housing Act 1996
- Family Law Act 1996
- Harassment Act 1997
- Crime and Disorder Act 1998 (Section 17)
- Human Rights Act 1998

It is important to get expert legal advice in order to find out how women and children may be protected against further abuse.

Children's Act 1989

The court can now attach an exclusion order (with power of arrest if necessary) permitting the removal of the suspected abuser from the home, rather than the child, for the protection of that child.

Housing Act 1996

Housing Associations and Local Authorities have the power to repossess properties as a result of nuisance or annoyance for which the tenant is responsible. Local Authorities may also apply for injunctions, to which a power of arrest can be attached, to protect tenants, in this case, women, from similar conduct.

Harassment Act 1997

The Protection from Harassment Act 1997 provides new protection under both the criminal and civil law by providing a link between the two. The provisions include two new criminal offences: the offence of criminal harassment and a more serious offence involving fear of violence. If convicted of either of these offences, there is an additional measure for protection: a restraining order can be granted by the court, prohibiting the offender from further similar conduct. Under the civil law there is also an injunction for prevention of harassment for those who are not eligible under Part IV of the Family Law Act 1996. These are women without children who do not live with their abusers.

Crime and Disorder Act 1998

This Act places a statutory duty on local partnerships to develop strategies to tackle and reduce the incidence of domestic violence. This is to highlight to perpetrators of domestic violence that their behaviour has a detrimental effect on neighbours and the community. The provision does not cover separated partners. Breach of Anti Social Behaviour Orders (ASBOs) under this order is a criminal offence punishable by a fine and/or imprisonment of up to five years. It helps assist the protection of women and children by curbing the anti-social behaviour of the abuser.

Family Law Act 1996

Part IV of the Family Law Act came into force in October 1997. It provides a set of remedies available in all courts with a family jurisdiction

to deal with domestic violence and the occupation of the family home. Orders available include non-molestation and occupation orders. A power of arrest must be attached to a non-molestation or occupation order where a court is satisfied that there has been actual or threatened violence against the applicant (the abused woman) by the respondent (her partner or family member).

The Human Rights Act 1998

The Human Rights Act 1998 is a new law in full force from 2 October 2000. Thus, the fundamental rights and freedoms in the European Convention on Human Rights (ECHR) are further safeguarded. This means that anyone who feels that their rights under the Convention have been breached can be dealt with as part of the UK's domestic law. There is no need to go to the European Court of Human Rights in Strasbourg since a case can be brought to a court in the UK.

There are sixteen basic rights in the Human Rights Act. The Act places on the state a positive duty to protect women and children experiencing domestic violence and abuse. Reasonable preventative operational measures must be taken by public authorities to protect women and children at risk from the criminal acts of their abuser.

- *To protect life (Article 2)*
- *To protect from torture, inhuman and degrading treatment (Article 3)*
- *To protect the right to respect for private and family life (Article 8)*

The Act cannot be used against a private individual who infringes the rights of another. The Human Rights law affects all other types of law and, therefore, it can be used to protect the rights of women and children experiencing domestic violence and abuse.

Police practice and response

In 1990, the Home Office issued a Circular to Chief Constables (Circular 60/90) instructing police that the immediate duty is to secure the protection of the 'victim' and any children, and then to consider the action against the offender (HMSO, 1990). This circular signalled that domestic violence is a crime and punishable by law. In 2000, the Home Office updated the guidance to reflect changes in police policy.

The police have an obligation to protect women and children experiencing domestic violence. Each police officer has the same powers to deal with domestic violence under common law, the Offences Against the Person Act 1861, or the Police and Criminal Evidence Act 1984 as they do in any other criminal assault or offence. The arrest of an abuser does not depend on the 'victim' consenting to formal proceedings taking place. Immediate action such as the arrest and removal of the abuser by police may be helpful for women to have the time and 'breathing space' to consider what they should do. The police are, however, encouraged to ensure that the perpetrators 'know' that they are held accountable when there is evidence of a crime.

■ The above information is reprinted with kind permission from Welsh Women's Aid – please visit www.welshwomensaid.org for more information, or see page 41 for their address details.

© Welsh Women's Aid

Perpetrators of domestic violence

Information from SupportLine

If you are violent in your relationship you are a perpetrator of domestic violence and need to accept that fact and try and get help. If you are being physically violent, emotionally abusing your partner, intimidating your partner, controlling your partner, sexually abusing your partner – you are a perpetrator of domestic violence.

Many perpetrators of domestic violence constantly put the blame on their partner – I'll stop hitting you if you do this – if you do that – if you stop winding me up – if you do what I say etc. etc. The only person who is responsible for your actions is YOU. By blaming others you are acting like a child – it is time to act like an adult and accept responsibility for your own actions. The time to get help is NOW – not to keep putting it off or denying that you need help. What you are doing is not only against the law but you are ultimately destroying another person, destroying their confidence, their trust, their self-esteem and their respect for you.

If you don't get help to stop what you are doing, this kind of behaviour will be carried on into all your relationships leaving broken relationships, unhappy relationships, fearful relationships for your partner. You have to want to get help for YOU, to be prepared to work hard on yourself and to face up to what you are doing and the damage you are causing your partner and also any children which may be involved in the relationship.

You may have been abusing your partner(s) for many years and got away with it as your partner has been too frightened to give evidence – the law is changing and the law will catch up with you. The police will be able to prosecute without always having evidence or a statement from your partner so you need to get help to stop abusing before it is too late and the choice will be taken out of your hands and your freedom taken away from you.

To be able to take responsibility for your actions and to stop blaming others takes strength and courage. Anyone who rules others through fear and intimidation is a cowardly, weak person. If you are a perpetrator of domestic violence you can choose what kind of person you want to be – cowardly and weak (blaming others for your actions and continuing your abusive behaviour) or strong and courageous (facing up to and taking responsibility for your actions and getting help). If you choose the latter then try and get help now – there are agencies who can provide workshops and counselling to help you to stop this cycle of abuse.

Anyone who rules others through fear and intimidation is a cowardly, weak person

■ The above information is provided courtesy of SupportLine – for details of agencies who can offer support and information to perpetrators of domestic violence, please visit their domestic violence page at www.supportline.org.uk/problems/domesticViolence.php, or call their helpline on (020) 8554 9004

© SupportLine

KEY FACTS

■ Domestic abuse or domestic violence is the term used to describe any abusive behaviour within an intimate relationship between two people. (page 1)

■ Many victims of abuse comment on how their partner is like a 'Jekyll and Hyde' – seems fine and lovely one moment or in public, but presents a completely different personality in private or at a different time. (page 2)

■ In the 2001/02 British Crime survey, 89% of the people who experienced more than four incidents of domestic violence were women. (page 4)

■ Domestic abuse is the summary of physically, sexually and psychologically abusive behaviours directed by one partner against another, regardless of their marital status or gender. Generally, when one form of abuse exists, it is coupled with other forms as well. (page 5)

■ Half of all homicides of women are killings by a partner or ex-partner. (page 7)

■ Prevalence surveys show that domestic violence takes place across class, race, age and social status. (page 8)

■ The BCS estimates that one in five (21%) women and one in ten (10%) men have experienced at least one incident of non-sexual domestic threat or force since they were 16. (page 9)

■ The total cost of domestic violence to services (criminal justice system, health, social services, housing, civil legal) amounts to £3.1 billion, while the loss to the economy is £2.7 billion. (page 10)

■ Abusers usually blame somebody else for their acts. They almost always have an excuse for their actions. (page 11)

■ Domestic violence in most towns and cities represents 25% of violent crime, but few men are prosecuted because women often fail to pursue their complaint. (page 13)

■ The most effective form of abuse is thought to be emotional, which is why men use not only physical violence but a combination of mental, verbal, economic and sexual abuse to control women. (page 15)

■ Of male victims of domestic abuse surveyed, 35% reported that the police had totally ignored what they had to say. 47% reported that they had been threatened with arrest despite being the victim. 21% said that they had been arrested despite being the victim. Only 3% reported that the violent female partner had been arrested. (page 17)

■ When questioned about how they'd react if physically assaulted for the first time by a current or future partner, 41 per cent of female adults say they'd leave straight away. (page 18)

■ A woman suffering domestic violence will be beaten an average of 35 times before finally calling the police. (page 18)

■ In half of the cases of violence between adults, children get hurt too. In nine out of ten cases, the child or children are in the same or next room when the violence is going on. (page 19)

■ More than half a million incidents (635,000) of domestic violence are reported in England and Wales each year. (page 19)

■ 150 years ago in the UK it was still legal for a man to beat his wife, as long as the stick was no thicker than his thumb. (page 22)

■ The Government definition of domestic violence is, 'any incident of threatening behaviour, violence or abuse – psychological, physical, sexual, financial or emotional – between adults who are or have been intimate partners or family members, regardless of gender or sexuality'. (page 24)

■ One in three child protection cases shows a history of domestic violence to the mother. Children living with domestic violence are three to nine times more likely to be injured and abused, either directly or while trying to protect a parent. (page 26)

■ Among teenagers aged 13-19 surveyed, more than four in 10 (43%) believed it was acceptable for a boyfriend to get aggressive in certain circumstances – for example if a girl cheated on him, flirted with somebody else, screamed at him or 'dressed outrageously'. One in six had been hit by a boyfriend, 4% of them regularly. (page 29)

■ Girls who grow up in homes where they are read bedtime stories identify with the book characters as role models. These characters provide them with a template for future submissive behaviour. (page 30)

■ Right now, 7,000 women and children are staying in refuges in England. Broaden the picture to the whole of the UK, and the annual figure for refuge-seekers is 63,000. (page 32)

■ One woman in four will experience domestic abuse during her lifetime – one woman in nine is experiencing domestic violence now. (page 32)

ADDITIONAL RESOURCES

You might like to contact the following organisations for further information. Due to the increasing cost of postage, many organisations cannot respond to enquiries unless they receive a stamped, addressed envelope.

Barnardo's
Tanners Lane
Barkingside
ILFORD
Essex
IG6 1QG
Tel: 020 8550 8822
Email:
media.team@barnardos.org.uk
Website: www.barnardos.org.uk
Barnardo's works with over 47,000 children, young people and their families in more than 300 projects across the county. This includes work with children affected by today's most urgent issues; homelessness, poverty, disability, bereavement and abuse.

Child and Women Abuse Studies Unit (CWASU)
University of North London
Ladbrook House
62-66 Highbury Grove
LONDON
N5 2AD
Tel: 020 7753 5037
Fax: 020 7753 3138
Email: cwas@unl.ac.uk
Website: www.cwasu.org
CWASU, originally The Child Abuse Studies Unit, was established in 1987 by two full-time staff of the then Polytechnic of North London – Mary MacLeod and Esther Saraga. Their concern at the time was to both develop feminist theory and practice, and take this perspective into professional training, especially that of social work.

ChildLine
Freepost 1111
LONDON
N1 0BR
Tel: 020 7753 5037
Fax: 020 7753 3138
Email: reception@childline.org.uk
Website: www.childline.org.uk
ChildLine is a free, national helpline for children and young people in trouble or danger. Provides confidential phone counselling service for any child

with any problem 24 hours a day. Children can call ChildLine on 0800 1111 (all calls are free of charge, 24 hours a day, 365 days a year).

Hidden Hurt
28 rue du Moulin
L-7621 LAROCHETTE
Luxembourg
Email: contact@hiddenhurt.co.uk
Website: www.hiddenhurt.co.uk
A site offering abuse information and support.

Mankind
Suite 367
Municipal Building
Corporation Street
TAUNTON, Somerset
TA1 4AQ
Tel: 01823 334244
Website: www.mankind.org.uk
Mankind draws attention to the problem of domestic abuse against men and its effect on families.

Refuge
2-8 Maltravers Street
LONDON
WC2R 3EE
Tel: 020 7395 7700
Fax: 020 7395 7721
Email: info@refuge.org.uk
Website: www.refuge.org.uk
Refuge provides accommodation and a unique range of professional, high quality services for over 650 abused women and children each year. If you are a woman needing advice or help call their 24-hour National Crisis Line on 0990 995443. Produces publications about Refuge's work and facts about domestic violence.

Royal College of Psychiatrists
17 Belgrave Square
LONDON
SW1X 8PG
Tel: 020 7235 2351
Email: rcpsych@rcpsych.ac.uk
Website: www.rcpsych.ac.uk
Produces an excellent series of free

leaflets on various aspects of mental health. Supplied free of charge but a stamped, addressed envelope is required.

University of Derby
Kedleston Road
DERBY
DE22 1GB
Tel: 01332 591041
Email: press-office@derby.ac.uk
Website: www.derby.ac.uk
A vibrant academic community committed to supporting people to maximise their potential.

Welsh Women's Aid
38-48 Crwys Road
CARDIFF
CF2 4NN
Tel: 029 20 390874
Fax: 029 20 390878
Website:
www.welshwomensaid.org
Welsh Women's Aid is the national network of local Women's Aid groups in Wales, which provides advice, information and temporary refuge for women and their children affected by domestic violence. Produces leaflets.

Women's Aid Federation of England (WAFE)
PO Box 391
BRISTOL
BS99 7WS
Tel: 0117 944 4411
Fax: 0117 924 1703
Email: info@womensaid.org.uk
Websites: www.womensaid.org.uk and www.thehideout.org.uk (for children and young people)
Provides advice, information and temporary refuge for women and their children who are threatened by mental, emotional or physical violence, harassment, or sexual abuse. Runs the Women's Aid National Domestic Violence Helpline: 08457 023 468. Mon-Thurs 10am-5pm; Fri 10am-3pm. Produces leaflets, books and resources.

ACKNOWLEDGEMENTS

The publisher is grateful for permission to reproduce the following material.

While every care has been taken to trace and acknowledge copyright, the publisher tenders its apology for any accidental infringement or where copyright has proved untraceable. The publisher would be pleased to come to a suitable arrangement in any such case with the rightful owner.

Chapter One: Domestic Violence

Domestic abuse, © Hidden Hurt, *Facts about domestic violence*, © The Women's Aid Federation of England 2005, *Types of abuse*, © Hidden Hurt, *Myths and facts*, © London Metropolitan University, *The extent of domestic violence*, © Crown Copyright is reproduced with permission of Her Majesty's Stationery Office 2004, *The cost of domestic violence*, © Crown Copyright is reproduced with permission of Her Majesty's Stationery Office, *Older women suffer domestic violence in silence*, © Help the Aged 2004, *Fighting back*, © Guardian Newspapers Ltd, *Why do women stay with violent men?*, © Justice for Women, *Violence people like to ignore*, © News Shopper 2004 – part of the Newsquest Media Group, a Gannett company, *Hidden victims*, © Mankind 2005, *Women say they'd walk . . .*, © The Women's Aid Federation of England 2004.

Chapter Two: Effects on Young People

Domestic violence, © ChildLine, *Why does domestic violence happen?*, © The Women's Aid Federation of England 2005, *Troubles at home kept secret by children*, © NSPCC 2004, *Silence is not always golden*, © NUT, *Domestic violence – in their words*, © Barnardo's, *Domestic violence – its effects on children*, © Royal College of Psychiatrists, *Alarm at acceptance of abuse by teenage girls*, © Guardian Newspapers Limited 2005, *And they all lived happily ever after …?*, © University of Derby.

Chapter Three: Getting Help

Freephone 24-hour National Domestic Violence Helpline, © The Women's Aid Federation of England 2004, *The safe house*, © iVillage Ltd, *Male victims of domestic violence*, © SupportLine, *Contacting Women's Aid*, © Welsh Women's Aid, *A friend in need*, © The Women's Aid Federation of England 2005, *How can I help my mum and dad?*, © The Women's Aid Federation of England 2005, *Legal protection against domestic abuse*, © Welsh Women's Aid, *Perpetrators of domestic violence*, © SupportLine.

Photographs and illustrations:

Pages 1, 24, 34: Don Hatcher; pages 4, 16, 26: Angelo Madrid; pages 8, 19: Bev Aisbett; pages 13, 22, 31, 37: Simon Kneebone; page 20: Andrew Smith; page 27: Pumpkin House.

Craig Donnellan
Cambridge
September, 2005